MORE FAVOURITE POEMS WE LEARNED IN SCHOOL

MORE FAVOURITE POEMS WE LEARNED IN SCHOOL

Chosen and Introduced
by
Thomas F Walsh

MERCIER PRESS

MERCIER PRESS

Trade enquiries to *CMD DISTRIBUTION*,
55a Spruce Avenue, Stillorgan Industrial Park, Blackrock, Dublin

© Introduction and Selection Thomas F Walsh

ISBN 1 85635 087 8

A CIP is available of this book from the British Library.

For Nuala

Acknowledgement

Thanks are due to the Literary Trustees of Walter de la Mare, and the Society of Authors as their representative for permission to print 'The Listeners' by Walter de la Mare.

Printed in Ireland by Colour Books Ltd.

Contents

An Innocent Heart

Introduction

Nobody was more amazed than I at the success of *Favourite Poems we Learned in School*, which is still a bestseller. For me it was a labour of love and as such I was happy to be engaged in putting the poems together and seeing them so well produced in book form: it was like finding a nice home for those you love! How foolish of me to think that I was somehow unique in treasuring the lines that linger in the mind and bring us back to the days of our childhood!

We are a part of all that we have met, I suppose, and poetry, thank goodness, is very much a part of what we are. Poetry came into being because of the needs of the heart. How often do lines learned in our formative years spring to mind again and take us back to the time when we first encountered them in our innocence and youth. Surely this is a good thing: surely a few great lines of noble verse is no great load to carry along this rough old road of life.

Previous generations of Irish men and women certainly found this to be true. They learned poetry by rote, but they learned to say it with great feeling and expression, and they also learned to love and appreciate great poetry. They could quote memorable lines and apt extracts from their lesson books not only because they learned them off by heart but also because they were inspired by them, strengthened by them, and comforted by them, too, when loneliness, sadness and grief knocked on their door. People will find comfort and support in their favourite poems: they will take encouragement and inspiration from the poems that have stood the test of time:

> Lives of great men all remind us
> We can make our lives sublime,
> And, departing, leave behind us
> Footprints on the sands of time.

It is remarkable to think that all the poetry contained in this little book was to be found in the Irish Primary School textbooks. Some of the poems would be quite difficult for a young mind to assimilate yet they had such strong rhyme and rhythm that the music and melody of the lines lodged in the memory and became part of the spirit. Many of the poems, too, had a story to tell, a lesson to impart, an ideal to inspire the learner. It is easier to remember something meaningful, and what gives us joy and pleasure remains in the memory long after the mundane and the insipid have been lost in the mist of passing years.

It was not without reason our parents and grandparents referred to their school books as 'Lesson Books'. I do not think there is a single poem here, however trivial it appears or how light in theme, but has some wisdom, some moral to impart. Such poems have, in the recent past, been castigated as being 'awash with sentiment', or 'moralistic' and therefore to be avoided like the plague. Perhaps it is time for a re-evaluation. We are very conscious, in the present age, of conserving all that is good and beautiful and valuable in our public buildings, our towns and cities and our physical environment in general. How much more important the things of the spirit; the values and sentiments and feelings that were important to our predecessors. What better vehicle for these than the poetry that our fathers and mothers loved and quoted to us as children.

The fact that so many people have enjoyed *Favourite Poems we Learned in School* shows, I suggest, that there is a great difference between what the literary critic tells us we *ought* to read and what we ourselves *want* to read. Nobody should knock poetry because it is sentimental or pragmatic. If it reminds us of lost innocence or if it inspires us when we need comfort then it is, I suggest, fulfilling one of its primary objectives. And if, in these poems, we find a sense of values that we all aspire to but do not always attain, then who can doubt their worth?

I found great pleasure in dusting off the old Lesson Books and jogging the memory of so many; it's great to know that the joy was shared. The poems in that volume were, as you know, all by Irish authors. Many people were disappointed not to see poems such as 'I Remember, I Remember', 'The Village Blacksmith', 'Psalm of Life', etc. Well, here you may find all the other poems you have half forgotten or whose names or poets you could not trace! I hope you get as much enjoyment out of it as you have, by all accounts, out of the first collection.

THOMAS F. WALSH

I Remember, I Remember

I Remember, I Remember

I remember, I remember
The house where I was born,
The little window where the sun
Came peeping in at morn;
He never came a wink too soon
Nor brought too long a day;
But now, I often wish the night
Had borne my breath away.

I remember, I remember
The roses, red and white,
The violets, and the lily-cups,
Those flowers made of light!
The lilacs where the robin built,
And where my brother set
The laburnum on his birthday –
The tree is living yet.

I remember, I remember
Where I used to swing,
And thought the air must rush as fresh
To swallows on the wing;
My spirit flew in feathers then
That is so heavy now,
And summer pools could hardly cool
The fever on my brow.

I remember, I remember
The fir tress dark and high;
I used to think their slender tops
Were close against the sky:
It was a childish ignorance,
But now 'tis little joy
To know I'm farther off from Heaven
Than when I was a boy.

Thomas Hood

The Retreat

Happy those early days, when I
Shined in my angel infancy!
Before I understood this place
Appointed for my second race,
Or taught my soul to fancy aught
But a white, celestial thought;
When yet I had not walked above
A mile or two, from my first love,
And looking back, at that short space,
Could see a glimpse of His bright face.

When on some gilded cloud or flower
My gazing soul would dwell an hour,
And in those weaker glories spy
Some shadows of eternity;
Before I taught my tongue to wound
My conscience with a sinful sound,
Or had the black art to dispense
A several sin to every sense,
But felt through all this fleshly dress
Bright shoots of everlastingness.

O how long I wander back,
And tread again that ancient track!
That I might once more reach that plain,
Where first I left my glorious train;
From whence the enlightened spirit sees
That shady city of palm trees.
But ah, my soul with too much stay
Is drunk, and staggers on the way.
Some men a forward motion love,
But I by backward steps would move;
And when this dust falls to the urn,
In that state I came, return.

Henry Vaughan

A Boy's Song

Where the pools are bright and deep,
Where the grey trout lies asleep,
Up the river and o'er the lea,
That's the way for Billy and me.

Where the blackbird sings the latest,
Where the hawthorn blooms the sweetest,
Where the nestlings chirp and flee,
That's the way for Billy and me.

Where the mowers mow the cleanest,
Where the hay lies thick and greenest –
There to trace the homeward bee,
That's the way for Billy and me.

Where the hazel bank is steepest,
Where the shadow lies the deepest,
Where the clustering nuts fall free,
That's the way for Billy and me.

James Hogg

The Village Blacksmith

Under the spreading chestnut tree
The village smithy stands;
The smith, a mighty man is he,
With large and sinewy hands;
And the muscles of his brawny arms
Are strong as iron bands.

His hair is crisp, and black, and long;
His face is like the tan;

16

His brow is wet with honest sweat,
He earns whate'er he can,
And looks the whole world in the face,
For he owes not any man.

Week in, week out, from morn till night,
You can hear his bellows blow;
You can hear him swing his heavy sledge,
With measured beat and slow,
Like a sexton ringing the village bell,
When the evening sun is low.

And children coming home from school
Look in at the open door;
They love to see the flaming forge,
And hear the bellows roar,
And catch the burning sparks that fly
Like chaff from a threshing floor.

He goes on Sunday to the church,
And sits among his boys;
He hears the clergy pray and preach,
He hears his daughter's voice
Singing in the village choir,
And it makes his heart rejoice.

It sounds to him like her mother's voice,
Singing in Paradise!
He needs must think of her once more,
How in the grave she lies;
And with his hard, rough hand he wipes
A tear out of his eyes.

Toiling, – rejoicing, – sorrowing,
Onward through life he goes;
Each morning sees some task begun,
Each evening sees its close;
Something attempted, something done,
Has earned a night's repose.

Thanks, thanks to thee, my worthy friend,
For the lesson thou hast taught!
Thus on the flaming forge of life
Our fortunes must be wrought;
Thus on its sounding anvil shaped
Each burning deed and thought.

Henry Wadsworth Longfellow

The Bridge

I stood on the bridge at midnight,
As the clocks were striking the hour,
And the moon rose over the city
Behind the dark church-tower.

I saw her bright reflection
In the water under me
Like a golden goblet falling
And sinking in the sea.

And far in the hazy distance
Of that lovely night in June,
The blaze of the flaming furnace
Gleamed redder than the moon.

Among the long black rafters
The wavering shadows lay,
And the current that came from the ocean
Seemed to lift and bear them away.

As, sweeping and eddying through them,
Rose the belated tide,
And, streaming into the moonlight,
The seaweed floated wide.

And like those waters rushing
Among the wooden piers,
A flood of thoughts came o'er me
That filled my eyes with tears.

How often, O how often,
In the days that had gone by,
I had stood on that bridge at midnight
And gazed on that wave and sky!

How often, O how often,
I had wished that the ebbing tide
Would bear me away on its bosom
O'er the ocean wild and wide!

For my heart was hot and restless,
And my life was full of care,
And the burden laid upon me
Seemed greater than I could bear.

But now it has fallen from me,
It is buried in the sea;
And only the sorrow of others
Throws its shadow over me.

Yet whenever I cross the river
On its bridge with wooden piers,
Like the odour of brine from the ocean
Comes the thought of other years.

And I think how many thousands
Of care-encumbered men,
Each bearing his burden of sorrow,
Have crossed the bridge since then.

I see the long procession
Still passing to and fro,
The young heart hot and restless,
And the old subdued and slow!

And for ever and for ever,
As long as the river flows,
As long as the heart has passions,
As long as life has woes,

The moon and its broken reflection
And its shadows shall appear,
As the symbol of love in heaven,
And its wavering image here.

Henry Wadsworth Longfellow

The Harper and His Dog

On the green banks of Shannon when Sheelagh was
   nigh,
No blithe Irish lad was so happy as I:
No harp like my own could so cheerily play,
And wherever I went was my poor dog Tray.

When at last I was forced from my Sheelagh to part,
She said, while the sorrow was big at her heart,
'Oh, remember your Sheelagh, when far, far away,
And be kind, my dear Pat, to your poor dog Tray.'

Poor dog, he was faithful and kind to be sure,
And he constantly loved me, although I was poor,
When the sour-looking folks sent me heartless away,
I had always a friend in my poor dog Tray.

When the road was so dark, and the night was so cold,
And Pat and his dog were grown weary and old,
How snugly we slept in my old coat of gray,
And he licked me for kindness, my poor dog Tray.

Though my wallet was scant, I remembered his case,
Nor refused my last crust to his pitiful face;

But he died at my feet on a cold winter's day,
And I played a lament for my poor dog Tray.

Where shall I go? Poor, forsaken and blind,
Can I find one to guide me so faithful and kind?
To my sweet native village, so far, far away,
I can never return with my poor dog Tray.

Thomas Campbell

Daisies

At evening when I go to bed
I see the stars shine overhead;
They are the little daisies white
That dot the meadows of the night.

And often while I'm dreaming so,
Across the sky the moon will go!
It is a lady sweet and fair,
Who comes to gather daisies there;

For when at morning I arise,
There's not a star left in the skies;
She's picked them all and dropped them down
Into the meadows of the town.

Frank Dempster Sherman

Farewell to the Farm

The coach is at the door at last;
The eager children, mounting fast
And kissing hands, in chorus sing:
Goodbye, goodbye to everything!

To house and garden, field and lawn,
To meadow-gates we swung upon,
To pump and stable, tree and swing,
Goodbye, goodbye to everything!

And fare you well for evermore,
O ladder at the hayloft door,
O hayloft where the cobwebs cling,
Goodbye, goodbye to everything!

Crack goes the whip, and off we go;
The trees and houses smaller grow;
Last, round the woody turn we swing:
Goodbye, goodbye to everything!

Robert Louis Stevenson

From a Railway Carriage

Faster than fairies, faster than witches,
Bridges and houses, hedges and ditches;
And charging along like troops in a battle,
All through the meadows the horses and cattle;
All of the sights of the hill and the plain
Fly as thick as driving rain;
And ever again, in the wink of an eye,
Painted stations whistle by.

Here is a child who clambers and scrambles,
All by himself and gathering brambles;
Here is a tramp who stands and gazes;
And there is the green for stringing the daisies!
Here is a cart run away in the road,
Lumping along with man and load;
And here is a mill, and there is a river:
Each a glimpse and gone for ever!

Robert Louis Stevenson

My Lost Youth

Often I think of the beautiful town
That is seated by the sea;
Often in thought go up and down
The pleasant streets of that dear old town,
And my youth comes back to me.
And a verse of a Lapland song
Is haunting my memory still:
'A boy's will is the wind's will,
And the thoughts of youth are long, long thoughts.'

I can see the shadowy lines of its trees,
And catch, in sudden gleams,
The sheen of the far-surrounding seas,
And islands that were the Hesperides
Of all my boyish dreams.
And the burden of that old song,
It murmurs and whispers still:
'A boy's will is the wind's will,
And the thoughts of youth are long, long thoughts.'

I remember the black wharves and the slips,
And the sea-tides tossing free;
And Spanish sailors with bearded lips,
And the beauty and mystery of the ships,
And the magic of the sea.
And the voice of that wayward song
Is singing and saying still:
'A boy's will is the wind's will,
And the thoughts of youth are long, long thoughts.'

I remember the bulwarks by the shore,
And the fort upon the hill;
The sunrise gun, with its hollow roar,
The drum-beat repeated o'er and o'er,
And the bugle wild and shrill.

And the music of that old song
Throbs in my memory still:
'A boy's will is the wind's will,
And the thoughts of youth are long, long thoughts.'

I remember the sea-fight far away,
How it thundered o'er the tide!
And the dead captains as they lay
In their graves, o'erlooking the tranquil bay
Where they in battle died.
And the sound of that mournful song
Goes through me with a thrill:
'A boy's will is the wind's will,
And the thoughts of youth are long, long thoughts.'

I can see the breezy dome of groves,
The shadows of Deering's Woods;
And the friendships old and the early loves
Come back with a Sabbath sound, as of doves
In quiet neighbourhoods.
And the verse of that sweet old song,
It flutters and murmurs still:
'A boy's will is the wind's will,
And the thoughts of youth are long, long thoughts.'

I remember the gleams and glooms that dart
Across the school-boy's brain;
The song and the silence in the heart,
That in part are prophecies, and in part
Are longings wild and vain.
And the voice of that fitful song
Sings on, and is never still:
'A boy's will is the wind's will,
And the thoughts of youth are long, long thoughts.'

There are things of which I may not speak;
There are dreams that cannot die;
There are thoughts that make the strong heart weak,
And bring a pallor into the cheek,

And a mist before the eye.
And the words of that fatal song
Come over me like a chill:
'A boy's will is the wind's will,
And the thoughts of youth are long, long thoughts.'

Strange to me now are the forms I meet
When I visit the dear old town;
But the native air is pure and sweet,
And the trees that o'ershadow each well-known street,
As they balance up and down,
Are singing the beautiful song,
Are sighing and whispering still:
'A boy's will is the wind's will,
And the thoughts of youth are long, long thoughts.'

And Deering's Woods are fresh and fair,
And with joy that is almost pain
My heart goes back to wander there,
And among the dreams of the days that were,
I find my lost youth again.
And the strange and beautiful song,
The groves are repeating it still:
'A boy's will is the wind's will,
And the thoughts of youth are long, long thoughts.'

Henry Wadsworth Longfellow

The Moon

The moon has a face like the clock in the hall;
She shines on thieves on the garden wall,
On streets and fields and harbour quays,
And birdies asleep on the forks of the trees.
The squalling cat and the squeaking mouse,
The howling dog by the door of the house,

The bat that lies in the bed at noon,
All love to be out by the light of the moon.
But all the things that belong to the day
Cuddle to sleep to be out of the way;
And flowers and children close their eyes
Till up in the morning the sun shall rise.

Robert Louis Stevenson

The Watchmaker's Shop

A street in our town
Has a queer little shop
With tumble-down walls
And a thatch on the top;
And all the wee windows
With crookedy panes
Are shining and winking
With watches and chains.

(All sorts and all sizes
In silver and gold,
And brass ones and tin ones
And new ones and old;
And clocks for the kitchen
And clocks for the hall,
High ones and low ones
And wag-at-the-wall).

The watchmaker sits
On a long-legged seat
And bids you the time
Of the day when you meet;
And round and about him
There's tickety-tock
From the tiniest watch
To the grandfather clock.

I wonder he doesn't
Get tired of the chime
And all the clocks ticking
And telling the time;
But there he goes winding
Lest any should stop,
This queer little man
In the watchmaker's shop.

Anonymous

The River of Life

The River of Life

The more we live, more brief appear
Our life's succeeding stages:
A day to childhood seems a year,
And years like passing ages.

The gladsome current of our youth,
Ere passion yet disorders,
Steals lingering like a river smooth
Along its grassy borders.

But as the care-worn cheek grows wan,
And sorrow's shafts fly thicker,
Ye Stars, that measure life to man,
Why seem your courses quicker?

When joys have lost their bloom and breath
And life itself is vapid,
Why, as we reach the Falls of Death,
Feel we its tide more rapid?

It may be strange – yet who would change
Time's course to slower speeding,
When one by one our friends have gone
And left our bosoms bleeding?

Heaven gives our years of fading strength
Indemnifying fleetness;
And those of youth, a seeming length,
Proportion'd to their sweetness.

Thomas Campbell

A Psalm of Life

Tell me not, in mournful numbers,
Life is but an empty dream! –
For the soul is dead that slumbers,
And things are not what they seem.

Life is real! Life is earnest!
And the grave is not its goal;
Dust thou art, to dust returnest,
Was not spoken to the soul.

Not enjoyment, and not sorrow,
Is our destined end or way;
But to act, that each tomorrow
Find us farther than today.

Art is long, and Time is fleeting,
And our hearts, though stout and brave,
Still, like muffled drums, are beating
Funeral marches to the grave.

In the world's broad field of battle,
In the bivouac of Life,
Be not like dumb, driven cattle!
Be a hero in the strife!

Trust no Future, howe'er pleasant!
Let the dead Past bury its dead!
Act – act in the living Present!
Heart within, and God o'erhead!

Lives of great men all remind us
We can make our lives sublime,
And, departing, leave behind us,
Footprints on the sand of time;

Footprints, that perhaps another,
Sailing o'er life's solemn main,
A forlorn and shipwrecked brother,
Seeing, shall take heart again.

Let us, then, be up and doing,
With a heart for any fate;
Still achieving, still pursuing,
Learn to labour and to wait.

Henry Wadsworth Longfellow

If

If you can keep your head when all about you
Are losing theirs and blaming it on you;
If you can trust yourself when all men doubt you,
But make allowance for their doubting too;
If you can wait and not be tired by waiting,
Or, being lied about, don't deal in lies,
Or, being hated, don't give way to hating,
And yet don't look too good, nor talk too wise;

If you can dream – and not make dreams your master;
If you can think – and not make thoughts your aim;
If you can meet with triumph and disaster
And treat those two impostors just the same;
If you can bear to hear the truth you've spoken
Twisted by knaves to make a trap for fools,
Or watch the things you gave your life to broken,
And stoop and build 'em up with worn-out tools;

If you can make one heap of all your winnings
And risk it on one turn of pitch-and-toss,
And lose, and start again at your beginnings
And never breathe a word about your loss;

If you can force your heart and nerve and sinew
To serve your turn long after they are gone,
And so hold on when there is nothing in you
Except the Will which says to them: 'Hold on';

If you can talk with crowds and keep your virtue,
Or walk with kings – nor lose the common touch;
If neither foes nor loving friends can hurt you;
If all men count with you, but none too much;
If you can fill the unforgiving minute
With sixty seconds' worth of distance run –
Yours is the Earth and everything that's in it,
And – which is more – you'll be a Man, my son!

Rudyard Kipling

Death the Leveller

The glories of our blood and state
Are shadows, not substantial things;
There is no armour against fate;
Death lays his icy hand on kings:
Sceptre and Crown
Must tumble down,
And in the dust be equal made
With the poor crooked scythe and spade.

Some men with swords may reap the field,
And plant fresh laurels where they kill:
But their strong nerves at last must yield;
They tame but one another still:
Early or late
They stoop to fate,
And must give up their murmuring breath
When they, pale captives, creep to death.

The garlands wither on your brow;
Then boast no more your mighty deeds!
Upon death's purple altar now
See where the victor-victim bleeds,
Your heads must come
To the cold tomb:
Only the actions of the just
Smell sweet, and blossom in their dust.

James Shirley

Lead Kindly Light

Lead, kindly light, amid the encircling gloom,
Lead Thou me on;
The night is dark, and I am far from home,
Lead Thou me on.
Keep Thou my feet: I do not ask to see
The distant scene; – one step enough for me.

I was not ever thus, nor prayed that Thou
Should lead me on;
I loved to choose and see my path; but now –
Lead Thou me on.
I loved the garish day; and, spite of fears,
Pride ruled my will; – remember not past years.

So long Thy power hath blest me, sure it still
Will lead me on –
O'er moor and fell, o'er crag and torrent, till
The night is gone –
And with the morn those angel-faces smile
Which I have loved long since, and lost awhile.

Cardinal J H Newman

Ring Out, Wild Bells

Ring out, wild bells, to the wild sky,
The flying cloud, the frosty light:
The year is dying in the night;
Ring out, wild bells, and let him die.

Ring out the old, ring in the new,
Ring, happy bells across the snow:
The year is going, let him go;
Ring out the false, ring in the true.

Ring out the grief that saps the mind,
For those that here we see no more;
Ring out the feud of rich and poor,
Ring in redress to all mankind.

Ring out a slowly dying cause,
And ancient forms of party strife;
Ring in the nobler modes of life,
With sweeter manners, purer laws.

Ring out the want, the care, the sin,
The faithless coldness of the times;
Ring out, ring out my mournful rhymes,
But ring the fuller minstrel in.

Ring out false pride in place and blood,
The civic slander and the spite;
Ring in the love of truth and right,
Ring in the common love of good.

Ring out old shapes of foul disease,
Ring out the narrowing lust of gold;
Ring out the thousand wars of old,
Ring in the thousand years of peace.

Ring in the valiant man and free,
The larger heart, the kindlier hand;
Ring out the darkness of the land,
Ring in the Christ that is to be.

From *Alfred Lord Tennyson's* 'In Memoriam'

I Envy Not in any Moods

I envy not in any moods
The captive void of noble rage,
The linnet born within the cage,
That never knew the summer woods:

I envy not the beast that takes
His license in the field of time.
Unfettered by the sense of crime,
To whom a conscience never wakes:

Nor, what may count itself as blest,
The heart that never plighted troth,
But stagnates in the weeds of sloth;
Nor any want-begotten rest.

I hold it true, whate'er befall;
I fell it, when I sorrow most;
'Tis better to have loved and lost
Than never to have loved at all.

From *Alfred Lord Tennyson's* 'In Memoriam'

A Wish

Mine be a cot beside the hill;
A bee-hive's hum shall soothe my ear;
A willowy brook that turns a mill,
With many a fall shall linger near.

The swallow, oft, beneath my thatch
Shall twitter from her clay-built nest;
Oft shall the pilgrim lift the latch,
And share my meal, a welcome guest.

Around my ivied porch shall spring
Each fragrant flower that drinks the dew;
And Lucy, at her wheel shall sing
In russet gown and apron blue.

The village-church among the trees,
Where first our marriage-vows were given,
With merry peals shall swell the breeze
And point with taper spire to Heaven.

Samuel Rogers

Solitude

Happy the man, whose wish and care
A few paternal acres bound,
Content to breathe his native air
In his own ground.

Whose herds with milk, whose fields with bread,
Whose flocks supply him with attire;
Whose trees in summer yield him shade,
In winter fire.

Blest, who can unconcern'dly find
Hours, days, and years, slide soft away
In health of body, peace of mind,
Quiet by day.

Sound sleep by night; study and ease
Together mixt, sweet recreation,
And innocence, which most does please
With meditation.

Thus let me live, unseen, unknown;
Thus unlamented let me die;
Steal from the world, and not a stone
Tell where I lie.

Alexander Pope

The Poplar Field

The poplars are fell'd; farewell to the shade
And the whispering sound of the cool colonnade;
The winds play no longer and sing in the leaves,
Nor Ouse on his bosom their image receives.

Twelve years have elapsed since I first took a view
Of my favourite field, and the bank where they grew;
And now in the grass behold they are laid,
And the tree is my seat that once lent me a shade!

The blackbird has fled to another retreat
Where the hazels afford him a screen from the heat;
And the scene where his melody charm'd me before
Resounds with his sweet-flowing ditty no more.

My fugitive years are all hasting away,
And I must ere long lie as lowly as they,

With a turf on my breast and a stone at my head,
Ere another such grove shall arise in its stead.

The change both my heart and my fancy employs;
I reflect on the frailty of man and his joys:
Short-lived as we are, yet our pleasures, we see,
Have a still shorter date, and die sooner than we.

William Cowper

Tomorrow

In the downhill of life, when I find I'm declining,
May my fate no less fortunate be
Than a snug elbow-chair will afford for reclining,
And a cot that o'erlooks the wide sea;
With an ambling pad-pony to pace o'er the lawn,
While I carol away idle sorrow,
And blithe as the lark that each day hails the dawn
Look forward with hope for Tomorrow.

With a porch at my door, both for shelter and shade,
As the sunshine or rain may prevail;
And a small spot of ground for the use of the spade,
With a barn for the use of the flail:
A cow for my dairy, a dog for my game,
And a purse when a friend wants to borrow;
I'll envy no Nabob his riches or fame,
Or what honours may wait him Tomorrow.

From the bleak northern blast may my cot be completely
Secured by a neighbouring hill;
And at night may repose steal upon me more sweetly
By the sound of a murmuring rill:
And while peace and plenty I find at my board,
With a heart free from sickness and sorrow,

With my friends may I share what Today may afford,
And let them spread the table Tomorrow.

And when I at last must throw off this frail cov'ring
Which I've worn for three-score years and ten,
On the brink of the grave I'll not seek to keep hov'ring,
Nor my thread wish to spin o'er again:
But my face in the glass I'll serenely survey,
And with smiles count each wrinkle and furrow;
As this old worn-out stuff, which is threadbare Today,
May become everlasting Tomorrow.

John Collins

Compassion

Teach me to feel another's woe,
To hide the fault I see;
That mercy I to others show
That mercy show to me.

Alexander Pope

Little, but Great

A traveller on a dusty road
Strewed acorns on the lea;
And one took root and sprouted up,
And grew into a tree.
Love sought its shade at evening-time,
To breathe its early vows;
And Age was pleased, in heats of noon,
To bask beneath its boughs.
The dormouse loved its dangling twigs,

The birds sweet music bore –
It stood a glory in its place,
A blessing evermore.

A little spring had lost its way
Amid the grass and fern;
A passing stranger scooped a well,
Where weary men might turn.
He walled it in, and hung with care
A ladle at the brink;
He thought not of the deed he did,
But judged that Toil might drink.
He passed again; and lo! the well,
By summer never dried,
Had cooled ten thousand parch'd tongues,
And saved a life beside.

A dreamer dropped a random thought,
'Twas old, and yet 'twas new –
A simple fancy of the brain,
But strong in being true;
It shone upon a genial mind,
And, lo! its light became
A lamp of life, a beacon ray,
A monitary flame.
The thought was small – its issue great:
A watch-fire on the hill,
It sheds its radiance far adown,
And cheers the valley still.

A nameless man, amid the crowd
That thronged the daily mart,
Let fall a word of hope and love,
Unstudied from the heart;
A whisper on the tumult thrown,
A transitory breath,
It raised a brother from the dust,
It saved a soul from death.
O germ! O fount! O word of love!

O thought at random cast!
Ye were but little at the first,
But mighty at the last!

Little by Little

One step and then another,
And the longest walk is ended;
One stitch and then another,
And the largest rent is mended;
One brick upon another,
And the highest wall is made;
One flake upon another,
And the deepest snow is laid.

Then do not look disheartened
O'er the work you have to do,
And say that such a mighty task
You never can get through;
But just endeavour, day by day,
Another point to gain;
And soon the mountain which you feared
Will prove to be a plain.

'Rome was not built within one day',
The ancient proverb teaches;
And Nature, by her trees and flowers,
The same sweet sermon preaches.
Think not of far-off duties,
But of duties which are near;
And, having once begun to work,
Resolve to persevere.

Anonymous

42

The Scholar and his Books

My days among the Dead are passed;
Around me I behold
Where'er these casual eyes are cast
The mighty minds of old:
My never-failing friends are they
With whom I converse day by day.

My thoughts are with the Dead; with them
I live in long-past years,
Their virtues love, their faults condemn,
Partake their hopes and fears,
And from their lessons seek and find
Instruction with a humble mind.

My hopes are with the Dead; anon
My place with them shall be,
And I with them shall travel on
Through all Futurity;
Yet leaving here a name, I trust,
That will not perish in the dust.

Robert Southey

Young and Old

When all the world is young, lad,
And all the trees are green
And every goose a swan, lad,
And every lass a queen;
Then hey for boot and horse lad,
And round the world away;
Young blood must have its course, lad,
And every dog his day.

When all the world is old lad,
And all the trees are brown,
And all the sport is stale, lad,
And all the wheels run down;
Creep home, and take your place there,
The spent and maimed among;
God grant you find a face there,
You loved when all was young.

Charles Kingsley

An Innocent Heart

A Child's Evening Prayer

Ere on my bed my limbs I lay,
God grant me grace my prayers to say!

O God preserve my mother dear
In health and strength for many a year!

And O preserve my father too,
And may I pay him reverence due!

And may I, my best thoughts employ
To be my parents hope and joy!

And O preserve my brothers both
From evil doings and from sloth!

And may we always love each other,
Our friends, our father, and our mother!

And still, O Lord, to me impart
An innocent and grateful heart,

That after my last sleep I may
Awake to Thy eternal day! Amen!

Samuel Taylor Coleridge

A Dutch Lullaby

Wynken, Blynken, and Nod one night
Sailed off in a wooden shoe –
Sailed on a river of misty light
Into a sea of dew.

'Where are you going, and what do you wish?'
The old moon asked the three.
'We have come to fish for the herring-fish
That live in this beautiful sea;
Nets of silver and gold have we,'
Said Wynken,
Blynken,
And Nod.

The old moon laughed and sung a song
As they rocked in the wooden shoe,
And the wind that sped them all night long
Ruffled the waves of dew;
The little stars were the herring-fish
That lived in the beautiful sea;
'Now cast your nets wherever you wish,
But never afeard are we' –
So cried the stars to the fishermen three,
Wynken,
Blynken,
And Nod.

All night long their nets they threw
For the fish in the twinkling foam,
Then down from the sky came the wooden shoe,
Bringing the fishermen home.
'Twas all so pretty a sail, it seemed
As if it could not be;
And some folks thought 'twas a dream they'd dreamed
Of sailing that beautiful sea.
But I shall name you the fishermen three:
Wynken,
Blynken,
And Nod.

Wynken and Blynken are two little eyes,
And Nod is a little head,
And the wooden shoe that sailed the skies
Is a wee one's trundle-bed;

So shut your eyes while mother sings
Of the wonderful sights that be,
And you shall see the beautiful things
As you rock in the misty sea
Where the old shoe rocked the fishermen three –
Wynken,
Blynken,
And Nod.

Eugene Field

Escape at Bedtime

The lights from the kitchen and parlour shone out
Through the blinds and the windows and bars;
And high overhead and all moving about
There were millions and millions of stars.

There ne'er were such thousands of leaves on a tree,
Nor of people in church or the park,
As the crowds of the stars that looked down upon me,
And glittered and winked in the dark.

The Dog and the Plough, and the Hunter, and all,
And the star of the sailor, and Mars,
These shone in the sky, and the pail by the wall
Would be half full of water and stars.

They saw me at last, and they chased me with cries,
And they soon had me packed into bed;
But the glory kept shining and bright in my eyes,
And the stars going round in my head.

Robert Louis Stevenson

A Tragic Story

There lived a sage in days of yore,
And he a handsome pigtail wore:
But wondered much, and sorrowed more,
Because it hung behind him.

He mused upon this curious case,
And swore he'd change the pigtail's place,
And have it dangling in his face,
Not dangling there behind him.

Says he, 'The mystery I've found –
I'll turn me round' – he turned him round;
But still it hung behind him.

Then round, and round, and out and in,
All day the puzzled sage did spin;
In vain – it mattered not a pin –
The pigtail hung behind him.

And right and left, and round about,
And up and down, and in and out
He turned; but still the pigtail stout
Hung steadily behind him.

And though his efforts never slack,
And though he twist, and twirl, and tack,
Alas! still faithful to his back,
The pigtail hangs behind him.

William Makepeace Thackeray

A Visit from St Nicholas

'Twas the night before Chrsitmas, when all through the
    house
Not a creature was stirring, not even a mouse;
The stockings were hung by the chimney with care,
In hopes that St Nicholas soon would be there;
The children were nestled all snug in their beds,
While visions of sugar-plums danced in their heads;
And mamma in her kerchief, and I in my cap,
Had just settled our brains for a long winter's nap –
When out on the lawn there arose such a clatter,
I sprang from my bed to see what was the matter.
Away to the window I flew like a flash,
Tore open the shutters and threw up the sash.
The moon on the breast of the new-fallen snow
Gave a lustre of midday to objects below;
When what to my wondering eyes would appear,
But a miniature sleigh and eight tiny reindeer,
With a little old driver, so lively and quick
I knew in a moment it must be St Nick.
More rapid than eagles his coursers they came,
And he whistled and shouted, and called them by name:
'Now, Dasher! now, Dancer! now, Prancer and Vixen!
On, Comet! on, Cupid! on, Donder and Blitzen!
To the top of the porch, to the top of the wall!
Now dash away, dash away, dash away all!'
As dry leaves that before the wild hurricane fly,
When they meet with an obstacle, mount to the sky,
So up to the house-top the coursers they flew,
With the sleigh full of toys – and St Nicholas too.
And then in a twinkling I heard on the roof
The prancing and pawing of each little hoof.
As I drew in my head, and was turning around,
Down the chimney St Nicholas came with a bound.
He was dressed all in fur from his head to his foot,
And his clothes were all tarnished with ashes and soot;

A bundle of toys he had flung on his back,
And he looked like a pedlar just opening his pack.
His eyes, how they twinkled! his dimples, how merry!
His cheeks were like roses, his nose like a cherry;
His droll little mouth was drawn up like a bow,
And the beard on his chin was as white as the snow.
The stump of a pipe he held tight in his teeth,
And the smoke it encircled his head like a wreath.
He had a broad face and a little round belly
That shook, when he laughed, like a bowl full of jelly,
He was chubby and plump – a right jolly old elf:
And I laughed, when I saw him, in spite of myself.
A wink of his eye and a twist of his head
Soon gave me to know I had nothing to dread.
He spoke not a word, but went straight to his work,
And filled all the stockings; then turned with a jerk,
And laying his finger aside of his nose,
And giving a nod, up the chimney he rose.
He sprang to his sleigh, to his team gave a whistle,
And away they all flew like the down of a thistle;
But I heard him exclaim, ere he drove out of sight,
'Happy Christmas to all, and to all a goodnight!'

Clement Clarke Moore

Bed-Time

The evening is coming,
The sun sinks to rest,
The rooks are all flying
Straight home to the nest.
'Caw!' says the rook, as he flies overhead,
'It's time little people were going to bed!'

The flowers are closing,
The daisy's asleep,

The primrose is buried
In slumber so deep.
Shut up for the night is the pimpernel red;
It's time little children were going to bed!

The butterfly, drowsy,
Has folded its wing;
The bees are returning,
No more the birds sing.
Their labour is over, their nestlings are fed;
It's time little children were going to bed!

Here comes the pony,
His work is all done,
Down through the meadow
He takes a good run.
Up go his heels, and down goes his head,
It's time little children were going to bed!

Good night, little people,
Good night and good night;
Sweet dreams to your eye-lids
Till dawning of light;
The evening has come; there's no more to be said;
It's time little children were going to bed!

Thomas Hood

Good Night and Good Morning

A fair little girl sat under a tree,
Sewing as long as her eyes could see;
Then smoothed her work, and folded it right,
And said: 'Dear work! Good night! Good night!'

Such a number of rooks came over her head,
Crying 'Caw! caw!' on their way to bed;

She said, as she watched their curious flight:
'Little black things! Good night! Good night!'

The horses neighed and the oxen lowed;
The sheep's 'Bleat! Bleat!' came over the road;
All seeming to say, with a quiet delight,
'Good little girl! Good night! Good night!'

She did not say to the sun 'Good night!'
Though she saw him there, like a ball of light;
For she knew that he had God's time to keep
All over the world, and never could sleep.

The tall pink foxglove bowed his head;
The violets curtsied, and went to bed;
And good little Lucy tied up her hair,
And said, on her knees, her favourite prayer.

And while on her pillow she softly lay,
She knew nothing more till again it was day;
And all things said to the beautiful sun,
Good morning! Good morning! our work is begun!'

Lord Houghton

Hiawatha's Childhood

By the shores of Gitche Gumee,
By the shining Big-Sea-Water,
Stood the wigwam of Nokomis
Daughter of the moon, Nokomis.
Dark behind it rose the forest,
Rose the black and gloomy pine-trees,
Rose the firs with cones upon them;
Bright before it beat the water,
Beat the clear and sunny water,

Beat the shining Big-Sea-Water.
   There the wrinkled old Nokomis
Nursed the little Hiawatha,
Rocked him in his linden cradle,
Bedded soft in moss and rushes,
Safely bound with reindeer sinews;
Stilled his fretful wail by saying,
'Hush! the Naked Bear will hear thee!'
Lulled him into slumber, singing,
'Ewa-yea! my little owlet!
Who is this, that lights the wigwam?
With his great eyes lights the wigwam!
Ewa-yea! my little owlet!'
   Many things Nokomis taught him
Of the stars that shine in heaven;
Showed him Ishkoodah, the comet,
Ishkoodah, with fiery tresses;
Showed the Death-Dance of the spirits,
Warriors with their plumes and war-clubs,
Flaring far away to northward
In the frosty nights of Winter;
Showed the broad white road in heaven,
Pathway of the ghosts, the shadows,
Running straight across the heavens,
Crowded with the ghosts, the shadows.
   At the door on summer evenings
Sat the little Hiawatha,
Heard the whispering of the pine-trees,
Heard the lapping of the water,
Sounds of music, words of wonder;
'Minne-wawa!' said the pine trees,
'Mudway-aushka!' said the water.
   Saw the fire-fly, Wah-wah-taysee,
Flitting through the dusk of evening,
With the twinkle of its candle
Lighting up the brakes and bushes,
And he sang the song of children,
Sang the song Nokomis taught him:
'Wah-wah-taysee, little fire-fly,

Little, flitting, white-fire insect,
Little, dancing white-fire creature
Light me with your little candle,
Ere upon my bed I lay me,
Ere in sleep I close my eyelids!'
  Saw the moon rise from the water,
Rippling, rounding from the water,
Saw the flecks and shadows on it,
Whispered, 'What is that, Nokomis?'
And the good Nokomis answered:
'Once a warrior, very angry,
Seized his grandmother, and threw her
Up into the sky at midnight;
Right against the moon he threw her;
'Tis her body that you see there.'
  Saw the rainbow in the heaven,
In the eastern sky, the rainbow,
Whispered, 'What is that, Nokomis?'
And the good Nokomis answered:
"Tis the heaven of flowers you see there;
All the wild-flowers of the forest,
All the lilies of the prairie,
When on earth they fade and perish,
Blossom in that heaven above us.'
  When he heard the owls at midnight,
Hooting, laughing in the forest,
'What is that?' he cried in terror,
'What is that,' he said, 'Nokomis?'
And the good Nokomis answered:
'That is but the owl and owlet,
Talking in their native language,
Talking, scolding at each other.'
  Then the little Hiawatha
Learned of every bird its language,
Learned their names and all their secrets,
How they built their nests in Summer,
Where they hid themselves in Winter,
Talked with them whene'er he met them,
Called them 'Hiawatha's Chickens'.

Of all the beasts he learned the language,
Learned their names and all their secrets,
How the beavers built their lodges,
Where the squirrels hid their acorns,
How the reindeer ran so swiftly,
Why the rabbit was so timid,
Talked with them whene'er he met them,
Called them 'Hiawatha's Brothers'.

Then Iagoo, the great boaster,
He the marvellous story-teller,
He the traveller and the talker,
He the friend of old Nokomis,
Made a bow for Hiawatha;
From a branch of ash he made it,
From an oak-bough made the arrows.
Tipped with flint, and winged with feathers,
And the cord he made of deer-skin.

Then he said to Hiawatha:
'Go, my son, into the forest,
Where the red deer herd together,
Kill for us a famous roebuck,
Kill for us a deer with antlers!'

Forth into the forest straightway
All alone walked Hiawatha
Proudly, with his bow and arrows;
And the birds sang round him, o'er him,
'Do not shoot us, Hiawatha!'
Sang the robin, the Opechee,
Sang the blue bird, the Owaissa,
'Do not shoot us, Hiawatha!'

Up the oak-tree, close behind him,
Sprang the squirrel, Adjidaumo,
In and out among the branches,
Coughed and chattered from the oak-tree,
Laughed, and said between his laughing,
'Do not shoot me, Hiawatha!'

And the rabbit from his pathway
Leaped aside, and at a distance
Sat erect upon his haunches,

Half in fear and half in frolic,
Saying to the little hunter,
'Do not shoot me, Hiawatha!'
   But he heeded not, nor heard them,
For his thoughts were with the red deer;
On their tracks his eyes were fastened,
Leading downward to the river,
To the ford across the river,
And as one in slumber walked he.
   Hidden in the alder-bushes,
There he waited till the deer came,
Till he saw two antlers lifted,
Saw two eyes look from the thicket,
Saw two nostrils point to windward,
And a deer came down the pathway,
Flecked with leafy light and shadow.
And his heart within him fluttered,
Trembled like the leaves above him,
Like the birch-leaf palpitated,
As the deer came down the pathway.
   Then, upon one knee uprising,
Hiawatha aimed an arrow;
Scarce a twig moved with his motion,
Scarce a leaf was stirred or rustled,
But the wary roebuck started,
Stamped with all his hoofs together,
Listened with one foot uplifted,
Leaped as if to meet the arrow;
Ah! the singing, fatal arrow,
Like a wasp it buzzed and stung him!
   Dead he lay there in the forest,
By the ford across the river;
Beat his timid heart no longer,
But the heart of Hiawatha
Throbbed and shouted and exulted,
As he bore the red deer homeward,
And Iagoo and Nokomis
Hailed his coming with applauses.
   From the red deer's hide Nokomis

Made a cloak for Hiawatha.
From the red deer's flesh Nokomis
Made a banquet in his honour.
All the village came and feasted,
All the guests praised Hiawatha,
Called him Strong-Heart, Soan-ge-taha!
Called him Lion-Heart, Mahn-ge-taysee!

Henry Wadsworth Longfellow

The May Queen

You must wake and call me early, call me early, mother
   dear;
Tomorrow'll be the happiest time of all the glad New Year;
Of all the glad New Year, mother, the maddest merriest
   day;
For I'm to be Queen o' the May, mother. I'm to be Queen o'
   the May.

There's many a black black eye, they say, but none so bright
   as mine;
There's Margaret and Mary, there's Kate and Caroline:
But none so fair as little Alice in all the land they say,
So I'm to be Queen o' the May, Mother, I'm to be Queen o'
   the May.

I sleep so sound all night, mother, that I shall never wake,
If you do not call me loud when the day begins to break:
But I must gather knots of flowers, and buds and garlands
   gay,
For I'm to be Queen o' the May, mother, I'm to be Queen o'
   the May.

As I came up the valley whom think ye should I see,
But Robin leaning on the bridge beneath the hazel-tree?
He thought of that sharp look, mother I gave him yesterday,

But I'm to be Queen o' the May, mother, I'm to be Queen o'
the May.

He thought I was a ghost, mother, for I was all in white,
And I ran by him without speaking, like a flash of light.
They call me cruel-hearted, but I care not what they say,
For I'm to be Queen o' the May, mother, I'm to be Queen o'
the May

They say he's dying for love, but that can never be:
They say his heart is breaking, mother – what is that to me?
There's many a bolder lad'll woo me any summer day,
And I'm to be Queen o' the May, mother, I'm to be Queen o'
the May.

Little Effie shall go with me tomorrow to the green,
And you'll be there, too, mother, to see me made the Queen;
For the shepherd lads on every side'll come from far away,
And I'm to be Queen o' the May, mother, I'm to be Queen o'
the May.

The honeysuckle round the porch has wov'n its wavy
bowers,
And by the meadow-trenches blow the faint sweet cuckoo-
flowers;
And the wild marsh-marigold shines like fire in swamps
and hollows gray,
And I'm to be Queen o' the May, mother, I'm to be Queen o'
the May.

The night-winds come and go, mother, upon the meadow-
grass,
And the happy stars above them seem to brighten as they
pass;
There will not be a drop of rain the whole of the livelong
day,
And I'm to be Queen o' the May, mother, I'm to be Queen o'
the May.

All the valley, mother'll be fresh and green and still,
And the cowlsip and the crowfoot are over all the hill,
And the rivulet in the flowery dale'll merrily glance and
    play,
For I'm to be Queen o' the May, mother, I'm to be Queen o'
    the May.

So you must wake and call me early, call me early, mother
    dear,
Tomorrow'll be the happiest time of all the glad New Year:
Tomorrow'll be of all the year the maddest merriest day,
For I'm to be Queen o' the May, mother, I'm to be Queen o'
    the May.

Alfred Lord Tennyson

Little Jesus

Little Jesus, wast thou shy
Once, and just as small as I?
And what did it feel like to be
Out of Heaven and just like me?
Did'st Thou sometimes think of there
And ask where all the angels were?
I should think that I would cry
For my house all made of sky:
I would look around the air
And wonder where my angels were.
Hadst Thou ever any toys,
Like us little girls and boys?
And didst Thou kneel at night to pray,
And didst Thou join Thy hands, this way?

So, a little Child, come down
And hear a child's tongue like Thy own;
Take me by the hand and walk,

And listen to my childish talk;
To Thy Father show my prayer
He will look, Thou art so fair,
And say, 'O Father, I, Thy Son,
Bring the prayer of a little one.'
And he will smile, that children's tongue
Has not changed since Thou wert young!

Francis Thompson

My Shadow

I have a little shadow that goes in and out with me
And what can be the use of him is more than I can see;
He is very, very like me from heel up to the head,
And I see him jump before me, when I jump into my bed.

The funniest thing about him is the way he likes to grow –
Not at all like proper children, which is always very slow;
For he sometimes shoots up taller like an India-rubber ball,
And he sometimes gets so little that there is none of him at
    all.

He hasn't got a notion of how children ought to play,
And can only make a fool of me in every kind of way;
He stays so close beside me, he's a coward you can see;
I'd think shame to stick to nursie as that shadow sticks to
    me.

One morning very early, before the sun was up,
I rose and found the shining dew on every buttercup;
But my lazy little shadow, like an errant sleepy-head,
Had stayed at home behind me, and was fast asleep in bed.

Robert Louis Stevenson

Over the Hill

'Traveller, what lies over the hill?
Traveller, tell to me;
I am only a child – from the window-sill
Over I cannot see.'

'Child, there's a valley over there,
Pretty, and wooded, and shy;
And a little brook that says, "Take care,
Or I'll drown you by and by!"'

'And what comes next?' 'A little town
And a towering hill again;
More hills and valleys, up and down,
And a river now and then.'

'And what comes next?' – 'A lonely moor,
Without a beaten way;
And a grey cloud sailing slow before
A wind that will not stay.'

'And then?' – 'Dark rocks and yellow sand
And a moaning sea beside.'
'And then?' – 'More sea, more sea, more land,
And rivers deep and wide.'

'And then?' – 'Oh, rock and mountain and vale,
Rivers and fields and men,
Over and over, a long, long tale –
And round to your home again.'

George MacDonald

The Little Elf

I met a little Elf-man once
Down where the lilies blow.
I asked him why he was so small,
And why he didn't grow.

He slightly frowned, and with his eye
He looked me through and through:
'I'm quite as big for me,' he said,
'As you are big for you.'

John Kendrick Bangs

The Swing

How do you like to go up in a swing,
Up in the air so blue?
Oh, I do think it the pleasantest thing
Ever a child can do!

Up in the air and over the wall,
Till I can see so wide,
Rivers and trees and cattle and all
Over the countryside –

Till I look down on the garden green,
Down on the roof so brown –
Up in the air I go flying again,
Up in the air and down!

Robert Louis Stevenson

To Stand and Stare

Leisure

What is this life if, full of care,
We have no time to stand and stare.

No time to stand beneath the boughs
And stare as long as sheep or cows.

No time to see, when woods we pass,
Where squirrels hide their nuts in grass.

No time to see, in broad daylight,
Streams full of stars, like skies at night.

No time to turn at Beauty's glance,
And watch her feet, how they can dance.

A poor life this if, full of care,
We have no time to stand and stare.

William H Davies

The Daffodils

I wandered lonely as a cloud
That floats on high o'er vales and hills,
When all at once I saw a crowd,
A host of golden daffodils;
Beside the lake, beneath the trees,
Fluttering and dancing in the breeze.

Continuous as the stars that shine
And twinkle on the Milky Way,
They stretch'd in never-ending line
Along the margin of a bay;

Ten thousand saw I at a glance
Tossing their heads in sprightly dance.

The waves beside them danced, but they
Out-did the sparkling waves in glee.
A poet could not but be gay
In such a jocund company!
I gazed – and gazed – but little thought
What wealth the show to me had brought:

For oft, when on my couch I lie
In vacant or in pensive mood,
They flash upon that inward eye
Which is the bliss of solitude;
And then my heart with pleasure fills,
And dances with the daffodils.

William Wordsworth

Ode to Autumn

Season of mists and mellow fruitfulness,
Close bosom-friend of the maturing sun;
Conspiring with him how to load and bless
With fruit the vines that round the thatch-eaves run,
To bend with apples the mossed cottage trees,
And fill all fruit with ripeness to the core;
To swell the gourd, and plump the hazel shells
With a sweet kernel; to set budding more,
And still more, later flowers for the bees,
Until they think warm days will never cease;
For Summer has o'erbrimmed their clammy cells.

Who hath not seen thee oft amid thy store?
Sometimes whoever seeks abroad may find
Thee sitting careless on a granary floor,
Thy hair soft-lifted by the winnowing wind;

Or on a half-reaped furrow sound asleep,
Drowsed with the fume of poppies, while they hook
Spares the next swath and all its twined flowers:
And sometimes like a gleaner thou dost keep
Steady thy laden head across a brook;
Or by a cyder-press, with patient look,
Thou watchest the last oozings, hours by hours.

Where are the songs of Spring? Ay, where are they?
Think not of them, thou hast thy music too –
While barred clouds bloom the soft-dying day
And touch the stubble-plains with rosy hue;
Then in a wailful choir the small gnats mourn
Among the river sallows, borne aloft
Or sinking as the light wind lives or dies;
And full-grown lambs bleat from hilly bourn;
Hedge-crickets sing; and now with treble soft
The red-breast whistles from a garden croft,
And gathering swallows twitter in the skies.

John Keats

Signs of Rain

The hollow winds begin to blow,
The clouds look black, the glass is low.

The soot falls down, the spaniels sleep,
The spiders from their cobwebs peep.

Last night the sun went pale to bed,
The moon in haloes hid her head.

The boding shepherd heaves a sigh,
For, see, a rainbow in the sky.

The walls are damp, the ditches smell,

Closed is the pink-eyed pimpernel.

Hark how the chairs and tables crack!
Old Betty's joints are on the rack.

Loud quack the ducks, the peacocks cry,
The distant hills are seeming nigh.

How restless are the snorting swine;
The busy flies disturb the kine.

Low o'er the grass the swallow wings,
The cricket, too, how sharp he sings.

Puss on the hearth with velvet paws,
Sits wiping o'er her whiskered jaws.

Through the clear stream the fishes rise,
And nimbly catch the incautious flies.

The glow-worms, numerous and bright,
Illumed the dewy dell last night.

At dusk the squalid toad was seen,
Hopping and crawling o'er the green.

The whirling wind the dust obeys,
And in the rapid eddy plays.

The frog has changed his yellow vest,
And in a russet coat is dressed.

Though June, the air is cold and still,
The mellow blackbird's voice is shrill.

My dog, so altered in his taste,
Quits mutton-bones on grass to feast.

And see yon rooks, how odd their flight,

They imitate the gliding kite;

And seem precipitate to fall,
As if they felt the piercing ball.

'Twill surely rain, I see with sorrow,
Our jaunt must be put off tomorrow.

Edward Jenner

The Brook

I come from haunts of coot and hern,
I make a sudden sally
And sparkle out among the fern,
To bicker down a valley.

By thirty hills I hurry down,
Or slip between the ridges,
By twenty thorps, a little town,
And half a hundred bridges.

Till last by Philip's farm I flow
To join the brimming river,
For men may come and men may go,
But I go on for ever.

I chatter over stony ways,
In little sharps and trebles,
I bubble into eddying bays,
I babble on the pebbles.

With many a curve my banks I fret
By many a field and fallow,
And many a fairy foreland set
With willow-weed and mallow.

I chatter, chatter, as I flow
To join the brimming river,

70

For men may come and men may go,
But I go on for ever.

I wind about, and in and out,
With here a blossom sailing,
And here and there a lusty trout,
And here and there a grayling,

And here and there a foamy flake
Upon me, as I travel,
With many a silvery waterbreak
Above the golden gravel,

And draw them all along, and flow
To join the brimming river,
For men may come and men may go,
But I go on for ever.

I steal by lawns and grassy plots,
I slide by hazel covers;
I move the sweet forget-me-nots
That grow for happy lovers.

I slip, I slide, I gloom, I glance,
Among my skimming swallows;
I make the nettled sunbeam dance
Against my sandy shallows.

I murmur under moon and stars
In brambly wildernesses;
I linger by my shingly bars;
I loiter round my cresses;

And out again I curve and flow,
To join the brimming river,
For men may come and men may go,
But I go on for ever.

Alfred Lord Tennyson

Night in Winter

Shut in from all the world without,
We sat the clean-winged hearth about,
Content to let the north-wind roar
In baffled rage at pane and door,
While the red logs before us beat
The frost-line back with tropic heat;
And ever, when a louder blast
Shook beam and rafter as it passed,
The merrier up its roaring draught
The great throat of the chimney laughed;
The house-dog on his paws outspread
Laid to the fire his drowsy head,
The cat's dark silhouette on the wall
A couchant tiger's seemed to fall;

What matter how the night behaved!
What matter how the north-wind raved!
Blow high, blow low, not all its snow
Could quench our hearth-fire's ruddy glow.

John Greenleaf Whittier

The Chase

The stag at eve had drunk his fill,
Where danced the moon on Monan's rill,
And deep his midnight lair had made
In lone Glenartney's hazel shade;
But, when the sun his beacon red
Had kindled on Benvoirlich's head,
The deep-mouth'd bloodhound's heavy bay
Resounded up the rocky way,
And faint, from farther distance borne,
Were heard the clanging hoof and horn.

As Chief, who hears his warder call,
'To arms! the foreman storm the wall,'
The antler'd monarch of the waste
Sprung from his heathery couch in hast.
But, ere his fleet career he took,
The dew-drops from his flanks he shook;
Like crested leader proud and high,
Toss'd his beam'd frontlet to the sky;
A moment gazed adown the dale,
A moment snuff'd the tainted gale,
A moment listen'd to the cry,
That thicken'd as the chase drew nigh;
Then, as the headmost foes appear'd,
With one brave bound the copse he clear'd,
And, stretching forward free and far,
Sought the wild heaths of Uam-Var.

Sir Walter Scott

The Ocean

There is a pleasure in the pathless woods,
There is a rapture on the lonely shore;
There is society where none intrudes –
By the deep sea – and music in its roar.
In these our interviews, from which I steal
From all I may be, or have been before,
To mingle with the universe and feel
What I can ne'er express – yet cannot all conceal.

Roll on, thou deep and dark blue ocean – roll!
Ten thousand fleets sweep over thee in vain;
Man marks the earth with ruin, – his control
Stops with the shore; – upon the watery plain
The wrecks are all thy deed, nor doth remain
A shadow of man's ravage, save his own,

When, for a moment, like a drop of rain,
He sinks into thy depths with bubbling groan,
Without a grave, unknell'd, uncoffin'd, and unknown.

The armaments which thunderstrike the walls
Of rockbuilt cities, bidding nations quake,
And monarchs tremble in their capitals;
The oak leviathians, whose huge ribs make
Their clay creator the vain title take
Of lord of thee, and arbiter of war, –
These are thy toys, and, as the snowy flake,
They melt into thy yeast of waves, which mar
Alike the Armada's pride, or spoils of Trafalgar.

Thy shores are empires, changed in all save thee: –
Assyria, Greece, Rome, Carthage, what are they?
Thy waters wasted them while they were free,
And many a tyrant since; their shores obey
The stranger, slave, or savage; their decay
Has dried up realms to deserts: – not so thou;
Unchangeable, save to thy wild waves' plain;
Time writes no wrinkle on thine azure brow;
Such as creation's dawn beheld, thou rollest now.

Lord Byron

The Wood-Cutter's Night Song

Welcome, red and roundy sun,
Dropping slowly in the West;
Now my hard day's work is done,
I'm as happy as the best.

Joyful are the thoughts of home,
Now I'm ready for my chair,
So, till morrow-morning's come,
Bill and mittens, lie ye there!

Though to leave your pretty song,
Little birds, it gives me pain,
Yet tomorrow is not long,
Then I'm with you all again.

So fare ye well! and hold your tongues,
Sing no more until I come;
They're not worthy of your songs
That never care to drop a crumb.

All day long I love the oaks,
But, at nights, yon little cot,
Where I see the chimney smokes,
Is by far the prettiest spot.

Wife and children all are there,
To revive with pleasant looks,
Table ready set, and chair,
Supper hanging on the hooks.

Welcome, red and roundy sun,
Dropping slowly in the west;
Now my hard day's work is done,
I'm as happy as the best.

John Clare

The Tiger

Tiger, tiger, burning bright
In the forests of the night,
What immortal hand or eye
Could frame thy fearful symmetry?

In what distant deeps or skies
Burnt the fire of thine eyes?

On what wings dare he aspire?
What the hand dare seize the fire?

And what shoulder and what art,
Could twist the sinews of thy heart?
And, when thy heart began to beat,
What dread hand and what dread feet?
What the hammer? what the chain?
In what furnace was thy brain?
What the anvil? what dread grasp
Dare its deadly terrors clasp?

When the stars threw down their spears,
And watered heaven with their tears,
Did He smile His work to see?
Did He who made the lamb make thee?

Tiger, tiger, burning bright
In the forests of the night,
What immortal hand or eye
Dare frame thy fearful symmetry?

William Blake

To the Cuckoo

O blithe new-comer! I have heard,
I hear thee and rejoice:
O Cuckoo! shall I call thee Bird,
Or but a wandering Voice?

While I am lying on the grass
Thy twofold shout I hear;
From hill to hill it seems to pass,
At once far off and near.

Though babbling only to the vale
Of sunshine and of flowers,
Thou bringest unto me a tale
Of visionary hours.

Thrice welcome, darling of the Spring!
Even yet thou art to me
No bird, but an invisible thing,
A voice, a mystery;

The same whom in my school-boy days
I listen'd to; that Cry
Which made me look a thousand ways
In bush, and tree, and sky.

To seek thee did I often rove
Through woods and on the green;
And thou wert still a hope, a love;
Still longed for, never seen!

And I can listen to thee yet;
Can lie upon the plain
And listen, till I do beget
That golden time again.

O blessed Bird! the earth we pace
Again appears to be
An unsubstantial, faery place,
That is fit home for thee!

William Wordsworth

Tales of Yore

Lucy Gray

Oft I had heard of Lucy Gray:
And, when I cross'd the wild,
I chanced to see at break of day
The solitary child.

No mate, no comrade Lucy knew;
She dwelt on a wide moor,
The sweetest thing that ever grew
Beside a human door!

You yet may spy the fawn at play,
The hare upon the green;
But the sweet face of Lucy Gray
Will never more be seen.

'Tonight will be a stormy night –
You to the town must go;
And take a lantern, Child, to light
Your mother through the snow.'

'That, father! will I gladly do:
'Tis scarcely afternoon –
The minster-clock has just struck two,
And yonder is the moon!'

At this the father raised his hook,
And snapp'd a faggot-band;
He plied his work; – and Lucy took
The lantern in her hand.

Not blither is the mountain roe:
With many a wanton stroke
Her feet disperse the powdery snow,
That rises up like smoke.

The storm came on before its time;
She wander'd up and down;
And many a hill did Lucy climb:
But never reach'd the town.

The wretched parents all that night
Went shouting far and wide;
But there was neither sound nor sight
To serve them for a guide.

At day-break on a hill they stood
That overlook'd the moor;
And thence they saw the bridge of wood
A furlong from their door.

They wept – and, turning homeward, cried
'In heaven we all shall meet!'
– When in the snow the mother spied
The print of Lucy's feet.

Then downwards from the steep hill's edge
They track'd the footmarks small;
And through the broken hawthorn hedge,
And by the long stone-wall:

And then an open field they cross'd:
The marks were still the same;
They tracked them on, nor ever lost;
And to the bridge they came:

They follow'd from the snowy bank
Those footmarks, one by one,
Into the middle of the plank;
And further there were none!

– Yet some maintain that to this day
She is a living child;
That you may see sweet Lucy Gray
Upon the lonesome wild.

O'er rough and smooth she trips along
And never looks behind;
And sings a solitary song
That whistles in the wind.

William Wordsworth

Casabianca

The boy stood on the burning deck, whence all, but he,
    had fled;
The flames, that lit the battle's wreck, shone round him
    o'er the dead.
Yet beautiful and bright he stood, as born to rule the
    storm;
A creature of heroic blood, a proud, though childlike
    form!

The flames rolled on – he would not go without his
    father's word;
That father, faint in death below, his voice no longer
    heard.
He called aloud: 'Say, father, say, if yet my task is done?'
He knew not that the chieftain lay, unconscious of his
    son.

'Speak, father!' once again he cried, 'if I may yet be
    gone?'
But now the booming shots replied, and fast the flames
    rolled on:
Upon his brow he felt their breath, and in his waving
    hair,
And looked from that lone post of death, in still, but
    brave despair,

And shouted but once more, aloud: 'My father, must I
    stay?'

While o'er him fast, through sail and shroud, the
   wreathing fires made way.
They wrapt the ship in splendour wild, they caught the
   flag on high,
They streamed above the gallant child, like banners in
   the sky.

Then came a burst of thunder-sound; – the boy – Oh!
   where was he?
Ask of the winds that far around, with fragments
   strewed the sea,
With mast and helm and pennon fair that well had borne
   their part:
But the noblest thing that perished there, was that young
   faithful heart.

Felicia Hemans

The Lady of Shalott

On either side the river lie
Long fields of barley and of rye,
That clothe the world and meet the sky;
And through the field the road runs by
To many-tower'd Camelot;
And up and down the people go,
Gazing where the lilies blow
Round an island there below,
The island of Shalott.

Willows whiten, aspens quiver,
Little breezes dusk and shiver
Thro' the wave that runs for ever
By the island in the river
Flowing down to Camelot.
Four gray walls, and four gray towers,

Overlook a space of flowers,
And the silent isle imbowers
The Lady of Shalott.

By the margin, willow-veil'd,
Slide the heavy barges trail'd
By slow horses; and unhail'd
The shallop flitteth silken-sail'd
Skimming down to Camelot:
But who hath seen her wave her hand?
Or at the casement seen her stand?
Or is she known in all the land,
The Lady of Shalott?

Only reapers, reaping early
In among the bearded barley,
Hear a song that echoes cheerly
From the river winding clearly,
Down to towered Camelot:
And by the moon the reaper weary,
Piling sheaves in uplands airy,
Listening, whispers, 'Tis the fairy
Lady of Shalott.'

II

There she weaves by night and day
A magic web with colours gay.
She has heard a whisper say,
A curse is on her if she stay
To look down to Camelot.
She knows not what the curse may be,
And so she weaveth steadily.
And little other care hath she,
The Lady of Shalott.

And moving thro' a mirror clear
That hangs before her all the year,
Shadows of the world appear.

There she sees the highway near
Winding down to Camelot:
There the river eddy whirls,
And there the surly village-churls,
And the cloaks of market girls
Pass onward from Shalott.

Sometimes a troop of damsels glad,
An abbot on an ambling pad,
Sometimes a curly shepherd-lad,
Or long-hair'd page in crimson clad,
Goes by to tower'd Camelot;
And sometimes thro' the mirror blue
The knights come riding two and two:
She hath no loyal knight and true,
The Lady of Shalott.

But in her web she still delights
To weave the mirror's magic sights,
For often thro' the silent nights
A funeral, with plumes and lights
And music, went to Camelot:
Or when the moon was overhead,
Came two young lovers lately wed;
'I am half sick of shadows,' said
The Lady of Shalott.

III

A bow-shot from her bower-eaves,
He rode between the barley-sheaves,
The sun came dazzling thro' the leaves,
And flamed upon the brazen greaves
Of bold Sir Lancelot.
A red-cross knight for ever kneel'd
To a lady in his shield,
That sparkled on the yellow field,
Beside remote Shalott.

The gemmy bridle glitter'd free,
Like to some branch of stars we see
Hung in the golden Galaxy.
The bridle bells rang merrily
As he rode down to Camelot:
And from his blazon'd baldric slung
A mighty silver bugle hung,
And as he rode his armour rung,
Beside remote Shalott.

And in the blue unclouded weather
Thick-jewell'd shone the saddle-leather,
The helmet and the helmet-feather
Burn'd like one burning flame together,
As he rode down to Camelot.
As often thro' the purple night,
Below the starry clusters bright,
Some bearded meteor, trailing light,
Moves over still Shalott.

His broad clear brow in sunlight glow'd;
On burnished hooves his war-horse trode;
From underneath his helmet flow'd
His coal-black curls as on he rode,
As he rode down to Camelot.
From the bank and from the river
He flash'd into the crystal mirror,
'Tirra lirra,' by the river
Sang Sir Lancelot.

She left the web, she left the loom,
She made three paces thro' the room,
She saw the water-lily-bloom,
She saw the helmet and the plume,
She look'd down to Camelot.
Out flew the web and floated wide;
The mirror crack'd from side to side:
'The curse is come upon me,' cried
The Lady of Shalott.

In the stormy east-wind straining,
The pale yellow woods were waning,
The broad stream in his banks complaining,
Heavily the low sky raining
Over tower'd Camelot;
Down she came and found a boat
Beneath a willow left afloat,
And round about the prow she wrote
The Lady of Shalott.

And down the river's dim expanse –
Like some bold seer in a trance,
Seeing all his own mischance –
With a glassy countenance
Did she look to Camelot.
And at the closing of the day
She loosed the chain, and down she lay;
The broad stream bore her far away,
The Lady of Shalott.

Lying, robed in snowy white
That loosely flew to left and right –
The leaves upon her falling light –
Thro' the noises of the night
She floated down to Camelot;
And as the boat-head wound along
The willowy hills and fields among,
They heard her singing her last song,
The Lady of Shalott.

Heard a carol, mournful, holy,
Chanted loudly, chanted lowly,
Till her blood was frozen slowly,
And her eyes were darkened wholly,
Turn'd to tower'd Camelot.
For ere she reach'd upon the tide
The first house by the water-side,

Singing in her song she died,
The Lady of Shalott.

Under tower and balcony,
By garden-wall and gallery,
A gleaming shape she floated by,
Dead-pale between the houses high,
Silent into Camelot.
Out upon the wharfs they came,
Knight and burgher, lord and dame,
And round the prow they read her name,
The Lady of Shalott.

Who is this? and what is here?
And in the lighted palace near
Died the sound of royal cheer;
And they cross'd themselves for fear,
All the knights at Camelot:
But Lancelot mused a little space;
He said: 'She has a lovely face;
God in His mercy lend her grace,
The Lady of Shalott.'

Alfred Lord Tennyson

Barbara Frietchie

Up from the meadows rich with corn,
Clear in the cool September morn,

The clustered spires of Frederick stand,
Green-walled by the hills of Maryland.

Round about them orchards sweep,
Apple and peach tree fruited deep,

Fair as a garden of the Lord
To the eyes of the famished rebel horde,

On that pleasant morn of the early fall,
When Lee marched over the mountain wall –

Over the mountains winding down,
Horse and foot, into Frederick town.

Forty flags with their silver stars,
Forty flags with their crimson bars,

Flapped in the morning wind: the sun
Of noon looked down and saw not one.

Up rose old Barbara Frietchie then,
Bowed with her fourscore years and ten,

Bravest of all in Frederick town,
She took up the flag the men hauled down;

In her attic window the staff she set,
To show that one heart was loyal yet.

Up the street came the rebel tread,
Stonewall Jackson riding ahead.

Under his slouched hat, left and right,
He glanced: the old flag met his sight.

'Halt!' – the dust-brown ranks stood fast.
'Fire!' – out blazed the rifle-blast.

It shivered the window, pane and sash;
It rent the banner with seam and gash,

Quick, as it fell from the broken staff,
Dame Barbara snatched the silken scarf.

She leaned far out on the window sill,
And shook it forth with a royal will.

'Shoot, if you must, this old grey head,
But spare your country's flag,' she said.

A shade of sadness, a blush of shame,
Over the face of the leader came;

The nobler nature within him stirred
To life at that woman's deed and word.

'Who touches a hair of yon grey head
Dies like a dog! March on!' he said.

All day long through Frederick street
Sounded the tread of marching feet;

All day long the free flag tossed
Over the heads of the rebel host.

Ever its torn folds rose and fell
On the loyal winds that loved it well;

And through the hill-gaps sunset light
Shone over it with a warm good-night.

Barbara Frietchie's work is o'er,
And the rebel rides on his raids no more.

Honour to her! and let a tear
Fall, for her sake, on Stonewall's bier.

Over Barbara Frietchie's grave,
Flag of Freedom and Union, wave!

Peace and order and beauty draw
Round thy symbol of light and law;

And ever the stars above look down
On thy stars below in Frederick Town.

John Greenleaf Whittier

Horatius on the Bridge

Just then a scout came flying,
All wild with haste and fear;
'To arms! to arms! Sir Consul:
Lars Porsena is here.'
On the low hills to westward
The consul fixed his eye,
And saw the swarthy storm of dust
Rise fast along the sky.

But the Consul's brow was sad,
And the Consul's speech was low,
And darkly looked he at the wall,
And darkly at the foe.
'Their van will be upon us
Before the bridge goes down;
And if they once may gain the bridge,
What hope to save the town?'

Then out spoke brave Horatius,
The Captain of the Gate:
'To every man upon this earth
Death cometh soon or late.
And how can man die better
Than facing fearful odds,
For the ashes of his fathers,
And the temples of his Gods!

'Hew down the bridge, Sir Consul,
With all the force ye may;
I with two more to help me,

Will hold the foe in play.
In yon strait path a thousand
May well be stopped by three.
Now who will stand on either hand,
And keep the bridge with me?'

Then up spake Spurius Lartius;
A Ramnian proud was he:
'Lo, I will stand on thy right hand,
And keep the bridge with thee.'
And out spake strong Herminius:
Of Titian blood was he:
'I will abide on thy left side,
And keep the bridge with thee.'

'Horatius,' quoth the Consul,
'As thou sayest, so let it be.'
And straight against the great array
Forth went the dauntless Three.
For Romans in Rome's quarrel,
Spared neither land nor gold,
Nor son nor wife, nor limb nor life,
In the brave days of old.

But meanwhile axe and lever
Have manfully been plied;
And now the bridge hangs tottering
Above the boiling tide.
'Come back, come back, Horatius!'
Loud cried the Fathers all.
'Back, Lartius! back, Herminius!'
Back, ere the ruin fall!'

Back darted Spurius Lartius;
Herminius darted back:
And, as they passed, beneath their feet
They felt the timbers crack.
But when they turned their faces,
And on the farther shore

Saw brave Horatius stand alone,
They would have crossed once more.

But with a crash like thunder
Fell every loosened beam,
And, like a dam, the mighty wreck
Lay right athwart the stream:
And a long shout of triumph
Rose from the walls of Rome,
As to the highest turret-tops
Was splashed the yellow foam.

Alone stood brave Horatius.
But constant still in mind;
Thrice thirty thousand foes before,
And the broad flood behind.
'Down with him!' cried false Sextus,
With a smile on his pale face.
'Now yield thee,' cried Lars Porsena,
'Now yield thee to our grace.'

Round turned he, as not deigning
Those craven ranks to see;
Nought spake he to Lars Porsena,
To Sextus nought spake he;
But he saw on Palatinus
The white porch of his home;
And he spake to the noble river
That rolls by the towers of Rome.

'Oh, Tiber! father Tiber!
To whom the Romans pray,
A Roman's life, a Roman's arms,
Take thou in charge this day!'
So he spake, and speaking sheathed
The good sword by his side,
And with his harness on his back,
Plunged headlong in the tide.

No sound of joy or sorrow
Was heard from either bank;
But friends and foes in dumb surprise,
With parted lips and straining eyes,
Stood gazing where he sank;
And when above the surges
They saw his crest appear,
All Rome sent forth a rapturous cry,
And even the ranks of Tuscany
Could scarce forbear to cheer.

But fiercely ran the current,
Swollen high by months of rain;
And fast his blood was flowing;
And he was sore in pain,
And heavy with his armour,
And spent with changing blows;
And oft they thought him sinking,
But still again he rose.

Never, I ween, did swimmer,
In such an evil case,
Struggle through such a raging flood
Safe to the landing place:
But his limbs were borne up bravely
By the brave heart within,
And our good father Tiber
Bore bravely up his chin.

And now he feels the bottom;
Now on dry earth he stands;
Now round him throng the Fathers
To press his gory hands;
And now, with shouts and clapping,
And noise of weeping loud,
He enters through the River-Gate,
Borne by the joyous crowd.

They gave him of the corn-land,
That was of public right,

As much as two strong oxen
Could plough from morn till night;
And they made a molten image,
And set it up on high,
And there it stands unto this day
So witness if I lie.

And in the nights of winter,
When the cold north winds blow,
And the long howling of the wolves
Is heard amidst the snow;
When round the lonely cottage
Roars loud the tempest's din,
And the good logs of Algidus
Roar louder yet within;

When the oldest cask is opened
And the largest lamp is lit;
When the chestnuts glow in the embers,
And the kid turns on the spit;
When young and old in circle
Around the firebrands close;
When the girls are weaving baskets,
And the boys are shaping bows;

When the goodman mends his armour,
And trims his helmet's plume;
When the goodwife's shuttle merrily
Goes flashing through the loom;
With weeping and with laughter
Still is the story told,
How well Horatius kept the bridge
In the brave days of old.

Lord Macaulay

Lochinvar

O, young Lochinvar is come out of the west,
Through all the wide Border his steed was the best;
And save his good broadsword he weapons had none,
He rode all unarm'd, and he rode all alone.
So faithful in love, and so dauntless in war,
There never was knight like the young Lochinvar.

He staid not for brake, and he stopp'd not for stone,
He swam the Eske river where ford there was none;
But ere he alighted at Netherby gate,
The bride had consented, the gallant came late:
For a laggard in love, and a dastard in war,
Was to wed the fair Ellen of brave Lochinvar.

So boldly he enter'd the Netherby hall,
Among bride's-men, and kinsmen, and brothers, and all:
Then spoke the bride's father, his hand on his sword,
(For the poor craven bridegroom said never a word,)
'O'come ye in peace here, or come ye in war,
Or to dance at our bridal, young Lord Lochinvar?'

'I long woo'd your daughter, my suit you denied; –
Love swells like the Solway, but ebbs like its tide –
And now am I come, with this lost love of mine,
To lead but one measure, drink one cup of wine.
There are maidens in Scotland more lovely by far,
That would gladly be bride to the young Lochinvar.'

The bride kiss'd the goblet: the knight took it up,
He quaff'd off the wine, and he threw down the cup.
She look'd down to blush, and she look'd up to sigh,
With a smile on her lips, and a tear in her eye.
He took her soft hand, ere her mother could bar,
'Now tread we a measure!' said young Lochinvar.

So stately his form, and so lovely her face,
That never a hall such a galliard did grace;
While her mother did fret, and her father did fume,
And the bridegroom stood dangling his bonnet and
    plume;
And the bride-maidens whisper'd, 'Twere better by far,
To have match'd our fair cousin with young Lochinvar.'

One touch to her hand, and one word in her ear,
When they reach'd the hall-door, and the charger stood
    near;
So light to the croupe the fair lady he swung,
So light to the saddle before her he sprung!
'She is won! we are gone, over bank, bush, and scaur;
They'll have fleet steeds that follow,' quoth young
    Lochinvar.

There was mounting 'mong Graemes of the Netherby
    clan;
Forsters, Fenwicks, and Musgraves, they rode and they
    ran:
There was racing and chasing, on Cannobie Lee,
But the lost bride of Netherby ne'er did they see.
So daring in love, and so dauntless in war,
Have ye e'er heard of gallant like young Lochinvar?

Sir Walter Scott

Ivan the Czar

He sat in silence on the ground,
The old and haughty Czar;
Lonely, though princes girt him round,
And leaders of the war;
He had cast his jewelled sabre,
That many a field had won,

To the earth beside his youthful dead,
His fair and first-born son.

With a robe of ermine for its bed
Was laid that form of clay,
Where the light a stormy sunset shed,
Through the rich tent made way;
And a sad and solemn beauty
On the pallid face came down,
Which the lord of nations mutely watched,
In the dust with his renown.

Low tones, at last, of woe and fear
From his full bosom broke;
A mournful thing it was to hear
How then the proud man spoke.
The voice that through the combat
Had shouted far and high,
Came forth in strange, dull, hollow tones,
Burdened with agony.

'There is no crimson on thy cheek,
And on thy lip no breath;
I call thee, and thou dost not speak –
They tell me this is death!
And fearful things are whispering
That I the deed have done –
For the honour of thy father's name,
Look up, look up, my son!

'Well might I know death's hue and mien, –
But on thine aspect, boy,
What, till this moment, have I seen,
Save pride and tameless joy?
Swiftest thou wert to battle.
And bravest there of all –
How could I think a warrior's frame
Thus like a flower should fall?

'I will not bear that still, cold look;
Rise up, thou fierce and free;
Wake as the storm wakes, I will brook
All, save this calm, from thee.
Lift brightly up and proudly
Once more thy kindling eyes!
Hath my word lost its power on earth?
I say to thee, Arise!

'Didst thou not know I loved thee well?
Thou didst not, and art gone
In bitterness of soul to dwell
Where man must dwell alone.
Come back, young fiery spirit,
If but for one hour, to learn
The secrets of the folded heart
That seemed to thee so stern.

'Thou wert the first, the first fair child,
That in mine arms I pressed;
Thou wert the bright one, that has smiled
Like summer on my breast.
I reared thee as an eagle;
To the chase thy steps I led;
I bore thee on my battle-horse;
I look upon thee – dead!

'Lay down my warlike banners here,
Never again to wave;
And bury my red sword and spear,
Chiefs, in my first-born's grave.
And leave! I have conquered;
I have slain; my work is done; –
Whom have I slain? Ye answer not;
Thou art too mute, my son.'

And thus his wild lament was poured
Through the dark, resounding night;
And the battle knew no more his sword,

Nor the foaming steed his might.
He heard strange voices moaning
In every wind that sighed;
From the searching stars of heaven he shrank;
Humbly the conqueror died.

Felicia Hemans

Little Hans

(The true story of an American boy who perished in a snowstorm while attempting to save the life of a little girl).

In the cosy chimney corner,
With his rosy cheeks aglow,
Little Hans was safely sheltered
From the driving hail and snow.
Back and forward went the mother
Dropping now and then a word,
While she paused to rock the cradle
Where the year-old baby stirred.

'Yes, my lad,' she softly answered
To a question of her son,
'Duty is the best of heroes,
Duty well and bravely done;
Never mind how hard, a hero
Faces hardness like a man.
God rewards the boy who ever
Does the very best he can.'

Came the day when, in a snowstorm,
Leaving school a mile away,
Little Hans with sturdy courage
Faced the dark and bitter day.
Gold-haired Mabel stood beside him:

'I will take her home,' he said,
Tying close the scarlet hood
About the sunny curly head.

Well, we know the hapless story,
How the children struggled on,
Whirled like drift-wood in a torrent,
Till the wintry light was gone;
Stumbling, sobbing, praying, calling,
In the darkness and the snow,
While the rescue parties sought them,
Waving torches to and fro:
While the mothers at the windows
Watched and waited, sick with dread,
And the frantic tempest battled
Like an army overhead.

When they found him Hans was sleeping,
With a smile upon his face,
Just as if an angel passing,
Lowly bent, had kissed the place;
Holding Mabel's dimpled fingers
Very tightly in his own,
His warm jacket for protection
O'er her little shoulders thrown.

Did the mother's heart remember,
Grieving for her hero lad,
What she said to him of duty?
Did she know how well he had
Done the noblest and the simplest
Work 'twas given him to do?
Dying in his happy childhood,
While his joyous life was new.

Mrs Sangster

101

Lord Ullin's Daughter

A Chieftain to the Highlands bound
Cries 'Boatman, do not tarry!
And I'll give thee a silver pound
To row us o'er the ferry!'

'Now who be ye, would cross Lochgyle,
This dark and stormy water?'
'O I'm the chief of Ulva's isle,
And this, Lord Ullin's daughter.

'And fast before her father's men
Three days we've fled together,
For should he find us in the glen,
My blood would stain the heather.

'His horsemen hard behind us ride –
Should they our steps discover,
Then who will cheer my bonny bride,
When they have slain her lover?'

Out spoke the hardy Highland wight,
'I'll go, my chief, I'm ready:
It is not for your silver bright,
But for your winsome lady: –

'And by my word! the bonny bird
In danger shall not tarry;
So though the waves are raging white
I'll row you o'er the ferry.'

By this the storm grew loud apace,
The water-wraith was shrieking;
And in the scowl of Heaven each face
Grew dark as they were speaking.

But still as wilder blew the wind,
And as the night grew drearer,
Adown the glen rode arméd men,
Their trampling sounded nearer.

'O haste thee, haste!' the lady cries,
'Though tempests round us gather;
I'll meet the raging of the skies,
But not an angry father.'

The boat has left a stormy land,
A stormy sea before her, –
When, oh! too strong for human hand
The tempest gather'd o'er her.

And still they row'd amidst the roar
Of waters fast prevailing:
Lord Ullin reach'd that fatal shore, –
His wrath was changed to wailing.

For, sore dismay'd, through storm and shade
His child he did discover: –
One lovely hand she stretch'd for aid,
And one was round her lover.

'Come back! come back!' he cried in grief,
'Across this stormy water:
And I'll forgive your Highland chief,
My daughter! – Oh, my daughter!'

'Twas vain: the loud waves lash'd the shore,
Return or aid preventing:
The waters wild went o'er his child,
And he was left lamenting.

Thomas Campbell

The Ship on Fire

There was joy in the ship as she furrowed the foam,
For fond hearts within were dreaming of home.
The young mother pressed fondly her babe to her breast,
And sang a sweet song as she rocked it to rest;
'Oh, happy!' said she, 'when our roaming is o'er,
We'll dwell in a cottage that stands by the shore!'

Hark! hark! what was that? Hark! hark! to the shout!–
'Fire! fire!' – then a tramp, and a rush and a rout;
And uproar of voices arose in the air,
And the mother knelt down, and the half-spoken prayer
That she offered to God, in her agony wild,
Was, 'Father, have mercy! Look down on my child!'

Fire! fire! it is raging above and below,
And the smoke and hot cinders all blindingly blow;
The cheek of the sailor grew pale at the sight,
And his eyes glistened wild in the glare of the light.
The flames in thick wreaths mounted higher and higher! –
O Heaven, it is fearful to perish by fire!

They prayed for the light, and, at noon-tide about,
The sun o'er the waters shone joyously out.
'A sail!' and they turned their glad eyes o'er the sea.
'They see us! they see us! the signal is waved!
They bear down upon us! – thank God! we are saved!'

Charles Mackay

The Wreck of the Hesperus

It was the schooner Hesperus,
That sailed the wintry sea;
And the skipper had taken his little daughter,
To bear him company.

Blue were her eyes as the fairy-flax,
Her cheeks like the dawn of day,
And her bosom white as the hawthorn buds
That ope in the month of May.

The skipper he stood beside the helm,
His pipe was in his mouth,
And he watched how the veering flaw did blow
The smoke now West, now South.

Then up and spake an old Sailor,
Had sailed the Spanish Main,
'I pray thee, put into yonder port,
For I fear a hurricane.

'Last night the moon had a golden ring,
And tonight no moon we see!'
The skipper he blew a whiff from his pipe,
And a scornful laugh laughed he.

Colder and colder blew the wind,
A gale from the North-east,
The snow fell hissing in the brine,
And the billows frothed like yeast.

Down came the storm, and smote amain
The vessel in its strength;
She shuddered and paused, like a frightened steed,
Then leaped her cable's length.

'Come hither! come hither! my little daughter,
And do not tremble so;
For I can weather the roughest gale
That ever wind did blow.'

He wrapped her warm in his seaman's coat
Against the stinging blast;
He cut a rope from a broken spar,
And bound her to the mast.

'O father! I hear the church-bell ring,
O say, what may it be?'
''Tis a fog-bell on a rock-bound coast!' –
And he steered for the open sea.

'O father I hear the sound of guns,
O say, what may it be?'
'Some ship in distress, that cannot live
In such an angry sea!'

'O father! I see a gleaming light,
O say, what may it be?'
But the father answered never a word,
A frozen corpse was he.

Lashed to the helm, all stiff and stark,
With his face turned to the skies,
The lantern gleamed through the gleaming snow
On his fixed and glassy eyes.

Then the maiden clasped her hands and prayed
That saved she might be;
And she thought of Christ, who stilled the wave
On the lake of Galilee.

And fast through the midnight dark and drear,
Through the whistling sleet and snow,
Like a sheeted ghost the vessel swept
Towards the reef of Norman's Woe.

And ever the fitful gusts between
A sound came from the land;
It was the sound of the trampling surf
On the rocks and the hard sea-sand.

The breakers were right beneath her bows,
She drifted a dreary wreck,
And a whooping billow swept the crew
Like icicles from her deck.

She struck where the white and fleecy waves
Looked soft as carded wool,
But the cruel rocks they gored her side
Like the horns of an angry bull.

Her rattling shrouds, all sheathed in ice,
With the masts went by the board;
Like a vessel of glass she stove and sank,
Ho! ho! the breakers roared!

At daybreak on the bleak sea-beach
A fisherman stood aghast,
To see the form of a maiden fair
Lashed close to a drifting mast.

The salt sea was frozen on her breast,
The salt tears in her eyes;
And he saw her hair, like the brown sea-weed,
On the billows fall and rise.

Such was the wreck of the Hesperus,
In the midnight and the snow!
Christ save us all from a death like this,
On the reef of Norman's Woe!

Henry Wadsworth Longfellow

Abou Ben Adhem

Abou Ben Adhem, may his tribe increase!
Awoke one night from a deep dream of peace
And saw, within the moonlight in his room,
Making it rich, and like a lily in bloom,
An angel writing in a book of gold: –

Exceeding peace had made Ben Adhem bold,
And to the presence in the room he said,
'What writest thou?' – The vision raised its head,
And with a look made of all sweet accord,
Answered, 'The names of those who love the Lord.'
'And is mine one?' said Abou. 'Nay, not so,'
Replied the angel. Abou spoke more low,
But cheerily still; and said, 'I pray thee then,
Write me as one that loves his fellow men.'

The angel wrote, and vanished. The next night
It came again with a great awakening light,
And showed the names whom love of God had blessed,
And lo! Ben Adhem's name led all the rest.

Leigh Hunt

The Listeners

'Is there anybody there?' said the Traveller,
Knocking on the moonlit door;
And his horse in the silence champed the grasses
Of the forest's ferny floor:
And a bird flew up out of the turret,
Above the Traveller's head:
And he smote upon the door again a second time;
'Is there anybody there?' he said.

But no one descended to the Traveller;
No head from the leaf-fringed sill
Leaned over and looked into his grey eyes,
Where he stood perplexed and still.
But only a host of phantom listeners
That dwelt in that lone house then
Stood listening in the quiet of the moonlight
To that voice from the world of men:
Stood thronging the faint moonbeams on the dark stair,
That goes down to the empty hall,
Hearkening in an air stirred and shaken
By the lonely Traveller's call.
And he felt in his heart their strangeness,
Their stillness answering his cry,
While his horse moved, cropping the dark turf,
'Neath the starred and leafy sky;
For he suddenly smote on the door, even
Louder, and lifted his head: –
'Tell them I came,' and no one answered,
That I kept my word,' he said.
Never the least stir made the listeners,
Though every word he spake
Fell echoing through the shadowiness of the still house
From the one man left awake:
Ay, they heard his foot upon the stirrup,
And the sound of iron on stone,
And how the silence surged softly backward,
When the plunging hoofs were gone.

                                        Walter de la Mare

War and Peace

Hohenlinden

On Linden, when the sun was low,
All bloodless lay the untrodden snow;
And dark as winter was the flow
Of Iser, rolling rapidly.

But Linden saw another sight,
When the drum beat at dead of night
Commanding fires of death to light
The darkness of her scenery.

By torch and trumpet fast array'd
Each horseman drew his battle-blade,
And furious every charger neigh'd
To join the dreadful revelry.

Then shook the hills with thunder riven;
Then rushed the steed, to battle driven;
And louder than the bolts of Heaven
Far flash'd the red artillery.

But redder yet that light shall glow
On Linden's hills of stainéd snow;
And bloodier yet the torrent flow
Of Iser, rolling rapidly.

'Tis morn; but scarce yon level sun
Can pierce the war-clouds, rolling dun,
Where furious Frank and fiery Hun
Shout in their sulphurous canopy.

The combat deepens. On, ye Brave
Who rush to glory, or the grave!
Wave, Munich! all thy banners wave,
And charge with all thy chivalry!

Few, few shall part, where many meet!
The snow shall be their winding-sheet,
And ever turf beneath their feet
Shall be a soldier's sepulchre.

Thomas Campbell

After Blenheim

It was a summer evening,
Old Kaspar's work was done,
And he before his cottage door
Was sitting in the sun;
And by him sported on the green
His little grandchild Wilhelmine.

She saw her brother Peterkin
Roll something large and round
Which he beside the rivulet
In playing there had found;
He came to ask what he had found
That was so large and smooth and round.

Old Kaspar took it from the boy
Who stood expectant by;
And then the old man shook his head,
And with a natural sigh
"Tis some poor fellow's skull,' said he,
'Who fell in the great victory.

'I find them in the garden
For there's many here about;
And often when I go to plough
The ploughshare turns them out.
For many thousand men,' said he,
'Were slain in that great victory.'

113

'Now tell us what 'twas all about,'
Young Peterkin he cries;
And little Wilhelmine looks up
With wonder-waiting eyes;
'Now tell us all about the war,
And what they fought each other for.'

'It was the English,' Kaspar cried,
'Who put the French to rout;
But what they fought each other for
I could not well make out.
But everybody said,' quoth he,
'That 'twas a famous victory.

'My father lived at Blenheim then,
Yon little stream hard by;
They burnt his dwelling to the ground,
And he was forced to fly;
So with his wife and child he fled,
Nor had he where to rest his head.

'With fire and sword the country round
Was wasted far and wide,
And many a childing mother then
And newborn baby died:
But things like that, you know, must be
At every famous victory.

'They say it was a shocking sight
After the field was won;
For many thousand bodies here
Lay rotting in the sun:
But things like that, you know, must be
After a famous victory.

'Great praise the Duke of Marlbro' won;
And our good Prince Eugene';
'Why 'twas a very wicked thing!'
Said little Wilhelmine;

'Nay ... nay ... my little girl,' quoth he,
'It was a famous victory.

'And everybody praised the Duke
Who this great fight did win.'
'But what good came of it at last?'
Quoth little Peterkin; –
'Why that I cannot tell,' said he,
'But 'twas a famous victory.'

Robert Southey

Land of our Birth

Land of our Birth, we pledge to thee
Our love and toil in the years to be,
When we are grown and take our place
As men and women with our race.

Father in Heaven, who lovest all,
Oh, help Thy children when they call;
That they may build from age to age,
An undefiléd heritage.

Teach us to bear the yoke in youth,
With steadfastness and careful truth;
That, in our time, Thy Grace may give
The Truth whereby the nations live.

Teach us to rule ourselves alway,
Controlled and cleanly night and day;
That we may bring, if need arise,
No maimed or worthless sacrifice.

Teach us to look in all our ends,
On Thee for judge, and not our friends;

That we, with Thee, may walk uncowed
By fear or favour of the crowd.

Teach us the Strength that cannot seek,
By deed or thought, to hurt the weak;
That, under Thee, we may possess
Man's Strength to comfort man's distress.

Teach us Delight in simple things,
And Mirth that has no bitter springs;
Forgiveness free of evil done,
And Love to all men 'neath the sun!

Land of our birth, our faith, our pride,
For whose dear sake our fathers died.
O Motherland, we pledge to thee
Head, heart and hand through the years to be.

Rudyard Kipling

Loss of the Royal George

Toll for the brave!
The brave that are no more!
All sunk beneath the wave
Fast by their native shore!

Eight hundred of the brave,
Whose courage well was tried,
Had made the vessel heel
And laid her on her side.

A land-breeze shook the shrouds
And she was overset;
Down went the Royal George,
With all her crew complete.

Toll for the brave!
Brave Kempenfelt is gone;
His last sea-fight is fought,
His work of glory done.

It was not in the battle;
No tempest gave the shock;
She sprang no fatal leak,
She ran upon no rock.

His sword was in its sheath,
His fingers held the pen,
When Kempenfelt went down
With thrice four hundred men.

Weigh the vessel up
Once dreaded by our foes!
And mingle with our cup
The tears that England owes.

Her timbers yet are sound,
And she may float again
Full charged with England's thunder,
And plough the distant main:

But Kempenfelt is gone,
His victories are o'er;
And he and his eight hundred
Must plough the wave no more.

William Cowper

Love of Country

Breathes there a man with soul so dead,
Who never to himself hath said,
This is my own, my native land!
Whose heart hath ne'er within him burned,
As home his footsteps he hath turned
From wandering on a foreign strand?
If such there breathe, go, mark him well;
For him no minstrel raptures swell;
High though his titles, proud his name,
Boundless his wealth as wish can claim,
Despite those titles, power and pelf,
The wretch, concentered all in self,
Living, shall forfeit fair renown,
And, doubly dying, shall go down
To the vile dust, from whence he sprung,
Unwept, unhonoured, and unsung.

Sir Walter Scott

The Destruction of Sennacherib

The Assyrian came down like a wolf on the fold,
And his cohorts were gleaming in purple and gold;
And the sheen of their spears was like stars on the sea,
When the blue wave rolls nightly on deep Galilee.

Like the leaves of the forest when summer is green,
That host with their banners at sunset were seen;
Like the leaves of the forest when autumn had blown,
That host, on the morrow, lay wither'd and strown.

For the angel of death spread his wings on the blast,
And breathed on the face of the foe as he pass'd;

And the eyes of the sleepers wax'd deadly and chill,
And their hearts but once heaved, and for ever grew
   still;

And there lay the steed with his nostril all wide,
But through it there roll'd not the breath of his pride;
And the foam of his gasping lay white on the turf,
And cold as the spray of the rock-beating surf.

And there lay the rider, distorted and pale,
With the dew on his brow and the rust on his mail;
And the tents were all silent, the banners alone,
The lances unlifted, the trumpet unblown.

And the widows of Ashur are loud in their wail,
And the idols are broke in the temples of Baal;
And the might of the Gentile, unsmote by the sword,
Hath melted like snow in the glance of the Lord!

Lord Byron

Tubal Cain

Old Tubal Cain was a man of might
In the days when Earth was young;
By the fierce red light of his furnace bright
The strokes of his hammer rung;
And he lifted high his brawny hand
On the iron glowing clear,
Till the sparks rushed out in scarlet showers,
As he fashioned the sword and spear.
And he sang – 'Hurra for my handiwork
Hurra for the spear and sword!
Hurra for the hand that shall wield them well,
For he shall be king and lord!'

To Tubal Cain came many a one,
As he wrought by his roaring fire,

119

And each one prayed for a strong steel blade
As the crown of his desire:
And he made them weapons sharp and strong,
Till they shouted loud for glee,
And gave him gifts of pearl and gold,
And spoils of the forest free.
And they sang – 'Hurra for Tubal Cain,
Who hath given us strength anew!
Hurra for the smith, hurra for the fire,
And hurra for the metal true!'

But a sudden change came o'er his heart,
Ere the setting of the sun,
And Tubal Cain was filled with pain
For the evil he had done;
He saw that men, with rage and hate,
Made war upon their kind,
That the land was red with the blood they shed
In their lust for carnage, blind.
And he said – 'Alas! that ever I made,
Or that skill of mine should plan,
The spear and the sword for men whose joy
Is to slay their fellow-man.'

And for many a day old Tubal Cain
Sat brooding o'er his woe;
And his hand forbore to smite the ore,
And his furnace smouldered low,
But he rose at last with a cheerful face,
And a bright courageous eye,
And bared his strong right arm for work,
While the quick flames mounted high.
And he sang – 'Hurra for my handicraft!'
And the red sparks lit the air;
'Not alone for the blade was the bright steel made,'
And he fashioned the first ploughshare.

And men, taught wisdom from the past,
In friendship joined their hands,

Hung the sword in the hall, the spear on the wall,
And ploughed the willing lands;
And sang – 'Hurra for Tubal Cain!
Our staunch good friend is he;
And for the ploughshare and the plough
To him our praise shall be.
But while oppression lifts its head,
Or a tyrant would be lord,
Though we may thank him for the Plough,
We'll not forget the Sword!'

Charles Mackay

Poems of Sadness

Little Boy Blue

The little toy dog is covered with dust,
But sturdy and staunch he stands;
The little toy soldier is red with rust,
And his musket moulds in his hands.
Time was when the little toy dog was new,
And the soldier was passing fair;
And that was the time when our Little Boy Blue
Kissed them and put them there.

'Now don't you go till I come,' he said,
'And don't you make any noise!'
Then, toddling off to his trundle-bed,
He dreamt of his pretty toys;
And, as he was dreaming, an angel song
Awakened our Little Boy Blue –
Oh! the years are many, the years are long,
But the little toy friends are true.

Aye, faithful to Little Boy Blue they stand,
Each in the same old place –
Awaiting the touch of a little hand,
The smile of a little face;
And they wonder, waiting the long years through,
In the dust of that little chair,
What has become of our Little Boy Blue,
Since he kissed them and put them there.

Eugene Field

Break, Break, Break

Break, break, break,
On thy cold grey stones, O Sea!
And I would that my tongue could utter
The thoughts that arise in me.

O well for the fisherman's boy,
That he shouts with his sister at play!
O well for the sailor lad,
That he sings in his boat on the bay!

And the stately ships go on
To their haven under the hill;
But O for the touch of a vanish'd hand,
And the sound of a voice that is still!

Break, break, break,
At the foot of thy crags, O Sea!
But the tender grace of a day that is dead
Will never come back to me.

Alfred Lord Tennyson

Over the Sea to Skye

Sing me a song of a lad that is gone,
Say, could that lad be I?
Merry of soul he sailed on a day
Over the sea to Skye.

Mull was astern, Rum on the port,
Eigg on the starboard bow;
Glory of youth glowed in his soul;
Where is that glory now?

125

Give me again all that was there,
Give me the sun that shone!
Give me the eyes, give me the soul,
Give me the lad that's gone.

Sing me a song of a lad that is gone,
Say, could that lad be I?
Merry of soul he sailed on a day
Over the sea to Skye.

Billows and breeze, islands and seas,
Mountains of rain and sun,
All that was good, all that was fair,
All that was me is gone.

Robert Louis Stevenson

Resignation

There is no flock, however watched and tended,
But one dead lamb is there!
There is no fireside, howsoe'er defended,
But has one vacant chair!

The air is full of farewells to the dying,
And mournings for the dead;
The heart of Rachel, for her children crying,
Will not be comforted!

Let us be patient! These severe afflictions
Not from the ground arise,
But oftentimes celestial benedictions
Assume this dark disguise.

We see but dimly through the mists and vapours;
Amid these earthly damps.

What seem to us but sad, funereal tapers
May be heaven's distant lamps.

There is no Death! What seems so is transition;
This life of mortal breath
Is but a suburb of the life elysian,
Whose portal we call Death.

She is not dead, the child of our affection, –
But gone unto that school
Where she no longer needs our poor protection,
And Christ himself doth rule.

In that great cloister's stillness and seclusion,
By guardian angels led,
Safe from temptation, safe from sin's pollution,
She lives, whom we call dead.

Day after day we think what she is doing
In those bright realms of air;
Year after year, her tender steps pursuing,
Behold her grown more fair.

Thus do we walk with her, and keep unbroken
The bond which nature gives,
Thinking that our remembrance, though unspoken,
May reach her where she lives.

Not as a child shall we again behold her;
For when with raptures wild
In our embraces we again enfold her,
She will not be a child;

But a fair maiden, in her Father's mansion,
Clothed with celestial grace;
And Beautiful with all the soul's expansion
Shall we behold her face.

And though at times impetuous with emotion
And anguish long suppressed,

The swelling heart heaves moaning like the ocean,
That cannot be at rest, –

We will be patient, and assuage the feeling
We may not wholly stay;
By silence sanctifying, not concealing,
The grief that must have way.

Henry Wadsworth Longfellow

Elegy Written in a Country Churchyard

The curfew tolls the knell of parting day,
The lowing herd wind slowly o'er the lea,
The ploughman homeward plods his weary way,
And leaves the world to darkness and to me.

Now fades the glimmering landscape on the sight,
And all the air a solemn stillness holds,
Save where the beetle wheels his droning flight,
And drowsy tinklings lull the distant folds.

Save that from yonder ivy-mantled tower
The moping owl does to the moon complain
Of such as, wandering near her secret bower,
Molest her ancient solitary reign.

Beneath those rugged elms, that yew-tree's shade,
Where heaves the turf in many a mouldering heap,
Each in his narrow cell forever laid,
The rude forefathers of the hamlet sleep.

The breezy call of incense-breathing morn,
The swallow twittering from the straw-built shed,

The cock's shrill clarion, or the echoing horn,
No more shall rouse them from their lowly bed.

For them no more the blazing hearth shall burn,
Or busy housewife ply her evening care;
No children run to lisp their sire's return,
Or climb his knees the envied kiss to share.

Oft did the harvest to their sickle yield,
Their furrow oft the stubborn glebe has broke;
How jocund did they drive their team afield!
How bowed the woods beneath their sturdy stroke!

Let not Ambition mock their useful toil,
Their homely joys and destiny obscure;
Nor Grandeur hear with a disdainful smile
The short and simple annals of the poor.

The boast of heraldry, the pomp of power,
And all that beauty, all that wealth e'er gave,
Awaits alike the inevitable hour: –
The paths of glory lead but to the grave.

Nor you, ye proud, impute to these the fault
If Memory o'er their tomb no trophies raise,
Where through the long-drawn aisle and fretted vault
The pealing anthem swells the note of praise.

Can storied urn or animated bust
Back to its mansion call the fleeting breath?
Can Honour's voice provoke the silent dust,
Or Flattery soothe the dull cold ear of death?

Perhaps in this neglected spot is laid
Some heart once pregnant with celestial fire;
Hands that the rod of empire might have swayed,
Or waked to ecstasy the living lyre:

But knowledge to their eyes her ample page
Rich with the spoils of time did ne'er unroll:

Chill Penury repressed their noble rage,
And froze the genial current of the soul.

Full many a gem of purest ray serene
The dark unfathomed caves of ocean bear;
Full many a flower is born to blush unseen,
And waste its sweetness on the desert air.

Some village Hampden, that with dauntless breast
The little tyrant of his fields withstood,
Some mute inglorious Milton here may rest,
Some Cromwell, guiltless of his country's blood.

The applause of list'ning senates to command,
The threats of pain and ruin to despise,
To scatter plenty o'er a smiling land,
And read their history in a nation's eyes,

Their lot forbad: nor circumscribed alone
Their growing virtues, but their crimes confined;
Forbad to wade through slaughter to a throne,
And shut the gates of mercy on mankind;

The struggling pangs of conscious truth to hide,
To quench the blushes of ingenuous shame,
Or heap the shrine of Luxury and Pride
With incense kindled at the Muse's flame.

Far from the madding crowd's ignoble strife
Their sober wishes never learned to stray;
Along the cool sequestered vale of life
They kept the noiseless tenor of their way.

Yet e'en these bones from insult to protect
Some frail memorial still erected nigh,
With uncouth rhymes and shapeless sculpture decked,
Implores the passing tribute of a sigh.

Their name, their years, spelt by th' unletter'd muse,
The place of fame and elegy supply:

And many a holy text around she strews,
That teach the rustic moralist to die.

For who to dumb Forgetfulness a prey
This pleasing anxious being e'er resigned,
Left the warm precincts of the cheerful day,
Nor cast one longing lingering look behind?

On some fond breast the parting soul relies,
Some pious drops the closing eye requires;
Even from the tomb the voice of Nature cries,
E'en in our ashes live their wonted fires.

For thee, who, mindful of the unhonoured dead,
Dost in these lines their artless tale relate;
If chance, by lonely contemplation led,
Some kindred spirit shall inquire thy fate,

Haply some hoary-headed swain may say,
'Oft have we seen him at the peep of dawn
Brushing with hasty steps the dews away,
To meet the sun upon the upland lawn;

'There at the foot of yonder nodding beech,
That wreathes its old fantastic roots so high,
His listless length at noontide would he stretch,
And pore upon the brook that babbles by.

'Hard by yon wood, now smiling as in scorn,
Muttering his wayward fancies he would rove,
Now drooping, woeful-wan, like one forlorn,
Or crazed with care, or crossed in hopeless love.

'One morn I missed him on the 'customed hill,
Along the heath, and near his favourite tree;
Another came; nor yet beside the rill,
Nor up the lawn, nor at the wood was he:

'The next with dirges due in sad array
Slow through the church-way path we saw him borne,

Approach and read (for thou canst read) the lay
Graved on the stone beneath yon aged thorn.'

The Epitaph:

Here rests his head upon the lap of Earth
A youth, to Fortune and to Fame unknown;
Fair Science frowned not on his humble birth,
And Melancholy marked him for her own.

Large was his bounty, and his soul sincere;
Heaven did a recompense as largely send:
He gave to Misery (all he had), a tear,
He gained from Heaven ('twas all he wished) a friend.

No farther seek his merits to disclose,
Or draw his frailties from their dread abode,
(There they alike in trembling hope repose,)
The bosom of his Father and his God.

Thomas Gray

She Dwelt Among the Untrodden Ways

She dwelt among the untrodden ways
Beside the springs of Dove;
A maid whom there were none to praise,
And very few to love.

A violet by a mossy stone
Half-hidden from the eye!
– Fair as a star, when only one
Is shining in the sky.

She lived unknown, and few could know
When Lucy ceased to be;

132

But she is in her grave, and oh,
The difference to me!

William Wordsworth

The Blind Boy

O say what is this thing call'd Light,
Which I must ne'er enjoy;
What are the blessings of the sight.
O tell your poor blind boy!

You talk of wondrous things you see,
You say the sun shines bright;
I feel him warm, but how can he
Or make it day or night?

My day or night myself I make
Whene'er I sleep or play;
And could I ever keep awake
With me 'twere always day.

With heavy sighs I often hear
You mourn my hapless woe;
But sure with patience I can bear
A loss I ne'er can know.

Then let not what I cannot have
My cheer of mind destroy;
Whilst thus I sing, I am a king,
Although a poor blind boy.

Colley Cibber

The Child's First Grief

'Oh, call my brother back to me!
I cannot play alone;
The summer comes with flower and bee –
Where is my brother gone?

'The butterfly is glancing bright
Across the sunbeam's track;
I dare not now to chase its flight –
Oh, call my brother back!

'The flowers run wild, the flowers we sowed
Around our garden tree;
Our vine is drooping with its load –
Oh, call him back to me!'

'He would not hear thy voice, fair child;
He may not come to thee;
The face that once like springtime smiled,
On earth no more thou'lt see.

'A rose's brief, bright life of joy,
Such unto him was given,
Go, thou must play alone, my boy,
Thy brother is in Heaven.'

'And has he left his birds and flowers,
And must I call in vain?
And through the long, long summer hours
Will he not come again?

'And by the brook, and in the glade,
Are all our wanderings o'er?
Oh, while my brother with me played,
Would I had loved him more!'

Felicia Hemans

The Death Bed

We watched her breathing thro' the night,
Her breathing soft and low,
As in her breast the wave of life
Kept heaving to and fro.

So silently we seem'd to speak,
So slowly moved about,
As we had lent her half our powers
To eke her living out.

Our very hopes belied our fears,
Our fears our hopes belied –
We thought her dying when she slept,
And sleeping when she died.

For when the morn came dim and sad
And chill with early showers,
Her quiet eyelids closed – she had
Another morn than ours.

Thomas Hood

The Sands of Dee

'O Mary, go and call the cattle home,
And call the cattle home,
And call the cattle home
Across the sands of Dee;'
The western wind was wild and dank with foam,
And all alone went she.

The western tide crept up along the sand,
And o'er and o'er the sand,

And round and round the sand,
As far as eye could see.
The rolling mist came down and hid the land:
And never home came she.

'Oh! is it weed, or fish, or floating hair –
A tress of golden hair,
A drownéd maiden's hair
Above the nets at sea?
Was never salmon yet that shone so fair
Among the stakes on Dee.'

They rowed her in across the rolling foam,
The cruel crawling foam,
The cruel hungry foam,
To her grave beside the sea:
But still the boatmen hear her call the cattle home
Across the sands of Dee.

Charles Kingsley

The Slave's Dream

Beside the ungathered rice he lay,
His sickle in his hand;
His breast was bare, his matted hair
Was buried in the sand.
Again, in the mist and shadow of sleep,
He saw his Native Land.

Wide through the landscape of his dreams
The lordly Niger flowed;
Beneath the palm-trees on the plain
Once more a king he strode;
And heard the tinkling caravans
Descend the mountain-road.

He saw once more his dark-eyed queen
Among her children stand;
They clasped his neck, they kissed his cheeks,
They held him by the hand! –
A tear burst from the sleeper's lids
And fell into the sand.

And then at furious speed he rode
Along the Niger's bank;
His bridle-reins were golden chains,
And, with a martial clank,
At each leap he could feel his scabbard of steel
Smiting his stallion's flank.

Before him, like a blood-red flag,
The bright flamingoes flew;
From morn till night he followed their flight,
O'er plains where the tamarind grew,
Till he saw the roofs of Caffre huts,
And the ocean rose to view.

At night he heard the lion roar,
And the hyena scream,
And the river-horse, as he crushed the reeds
Beside some hidden stream;
And it passed, like a glorious roll of drums,
Through the triumph of his dream.

The forests, with their myriad tongues,
Shouted of liberty;
And the Blast of the Desert cried aloud,
With a voice so wild and free,
That he started in his sleep and smiled
At their tempestuous glee.

He did not feel the driver's whip,
Nor the burning heat of day;
For Death had illumined the Land of Sleep,
And his lifeless body lay

A worn-out fetter, that the soul
Had broken and thrown away!

Henry Wadsworth Longfellow

Requiem

Under the wide and starry sky,
Dig the grave and let me lie.
Glad did I live and gladly die,
And I laid me down with a will.

This be the verse you grave for me:
Here he lies where he longed to be;
Home is the sailor, home from the sea,
And the hunter home from the hill.

Robert Louis Stevenson

Crossing the Bar

Sunset and evening star,
And one clear call for me!
And may there be no moaning of the bar,
When I put out to sea.

But such a tide as moving seems asleep,
Too full for sound and foam,
When that which drew from out the boundless deep
Turns home.

Twilight and evening bell,
And after that the dark!

138

And may there be no sadness of farewell,
When I embark;

For tho' from out our bourne of Time and Place
The flood may bear me far,
I hope to see my Pilot face to face
When I have crost the bar.

Alfred Lord Tennyson

All the World's a Stage

Selections from

William Shakespeare

from *The Merchant of Venice*

Lorenzo: How sweet the moonlight sleeps upon this bank!
Here will we sit, and let the sounds of music
Creep in our ears: soft stillness and the night
Become the touches of sweet harmony.
Sit, Jessica: look, how the floor of heaven
Is thick inlaid with patines of bright gold:
There's not the smallest orb which thou behold'st
But in his motion like an angel sings,
Still quiring to the young-eyed cherubims;
Such harmony is in immortal souls;
But, whilst this muddy vesture of decay
Doth grossly close it in, we cannot hear it. –
(Enter Musicians)
Come, ho! and wake Diana with a hymn;
With sweetest touches pierce your mistress' ear,
And draw her home with music.
Jessica: I am never merry when I hear sweet music.
Lorenzo: The reason is, your spirits are attentive:
For do but note a wild and wanton herd,
Or race of youthful and unhandled colts,
Fetching mad bounds, bellowing, and neighing loud,
Which is the hot condition of their blood;
If they but hear perchance a trumpet sound,
Or any air of music touch their ears,
You shall perceive them make a mutual stand.

from *Antony and Cleopatra*

The barge she sat in, like a burnish'd throne,
Burn'd on the water; the poop was beaten gold,
Purple the sails, and so perfumed, that
The winds were love-sick with them, the oars were

142

    silver,
Which to the tune of flutes kept stroke, and made
The water which they beat to follow faster,
As amorous of their strokes. For her own person,
It beggar'd description; she did lie
In her pavilion, – cloth-of-gold of tissue, –
O'er-picturing that Venus where we see
The fancy outwork nature; on each side her
Stood pretty-dimpled boys, like smiling Cupids,
With divers-colour'd fans, whose wind did seem
To glow the delicate cheeks which they did cool,
And what they undid did.

from *Julius Caesar*

Antony: Friends, Romans, countrymen, lend me your ears;
    I come to bury Caesar, not to praise him.
    The evil that men do lives after them;
    The good is oft interred with their bones;
    So let it be with Caesar. The noble Brutus
    Hath told you Caesar was ambitious.
    If it was so, it was a grievous fault,
    And grievously hath Caesar answer'd it.
    Here, under leave of Brutus and the rest –
    For Brutus is an honourable man;
    So are they all, all honourable men –
    Come I to speak in Caesar's funeral.
    He was my friend, faithful and just to me:
    But Brutus is an honourable man.
    He hath brought many captives home to Rome,
    Whose ransoms did the general coffers fill:
    Did this in Caesar seem ambitious?
    When that the poor have cried, Caesar hath wept:
    Ambition should be made of sterner stuff:
    Yet Brutus says he was ambitious;

And Brutus is an honourable man.
You all did see, that, on the Lupercal,
I thrice presented him a kingly crown,
Which he did thrice refuse: was this ambition?
Yet Brutus says he was ambitious;
And, sure, he is an honourable man!
I speak not to disprove what Brutus spoke;
But here I am to speak what I do know.
You all did love him once, not without cause:
What cause withholds you, then, to mourn for him?
O judgement! thou art fled to brutish beasts,
And men have lost their reason! – Bear with me:
My heart is in the coffin there with Caesar;
And I must pause till it come back to me.

from *The Merchant of Venice*

The quality of mercy is not strain'd;
It droppeth, as the gentle rain from heaven,
Upon the place beneath; it is twice bless'd-
It blesseth him that gives, and him that takes:
'Tis mightiest in the mightiest; it becomes
The throned monarch better than his crown;
His sceptre shews the force of temporal power,
The attribute to awe and majesty,
Wherein doth sit the dread and fear of kings;
But mercy is above this sceptr'd sway,
It is an attribute to God Himself;
And earthly power doth then shew likest God's,
When mercy seasons justice. Therefore, Jew,
Though justice be thy plea, consider this –
That in the course of justice, none of us
Should see salvation. We do pray for mercy;
And that same prayer doth teach us all to render
The deeds of mercy. I have spoke thus much
To mitigate the justice of the plea;

Which if thou follow, this strict court of Venice
Must needs give sentence 'gainst the merchant there.

from *King Henry VIII*

Wolsey: Farewell! a long farewell, to all my greatness!
　　This is the state of man: today he puts forth
　　The tender leaves of hope; tomorrow blossoms,
　　And bears his blushing honours thick upon him;
　　The third day comes a frost, a killing frost;
　　And, when he thinks, good easy man, full surely
　　His greatness is a-ripening, nips his root,
　　And then he falls, as I do. I have ventur'd,
　　Like little wanton boys that swim on bladders,
　　This many summers in a sea of glory,
　　But far beyond my depth: my highblown pride
　　At length broke under me, and now has left me
　　Weary and old with service, to the mercy
　　Of a rude stream that must forever hide me.
　　Vain pomp and glory of this world, I hate ye:
　　I feel my heart new open'd. O how wretched
　　Is that poor man that hangs on princes' favours!
　　There is, betwixt that smile we would aspire to,
　　That sweet aspect of princes, and their ruin,
　　More pangs and fears than wars or women have;
　　And when he falls, he falls like Lucifer,
　　Never to hope again.

from *Othello*

Good name in man and woman, dear my lord,
Is the immediate jewel of their souls;
Who steals my purse steals trash; 'tis something,
    nothing;
'Twas mine, 'tis his, and has been slave to thousands;
But he that filches from me my good name
Robs me of that which not enriches him,
And makes me poor indeed.

from *Measure for Measure*

There is a kind of character in thy life,
That, to the observer, doth thy history
Fully unfold; thyself and thy belongings
Are not thine own so proper, as to waste
Thyself upon thy virtues, them on thee.
Heaven doth with us, as we with torches do;
Not light them for themselves: for if our virtues
Did not go forth of us, 'Twere all alike
As if we had them not. Spirits are not finely touch'd,
But to fine issues: nor nature never lends
The smallest scruple of her excellence,
But, like a thrifty goddess, she determines
Herself the glory of a creditor,
Both thanks and use.

from *Measure for Measure*

Ay, but to die, and go we know not where;
To lie in cold obstruction and to rot:
This sensible warm motion to become
A kneaded clod; and the delighted spirit
To bathe in fiery floods, or to reside
In thrilling regions of thick-ribbed ice;
To be imprisoned in the viewless winds,
And blown with restless violence round about
The pendent world; or to be worse than worst
Of those, that lawless and incertain thoughts
Imagine howling! – 'tis too horrible!
The weariest and most loathed worldly life,
That age, ache, penury and imprisonment
Can lay on nature, is a paradise
To what we fear of death.

from *King John*

To gild refined gold, to paint the lily,
To throw a perfume on the violet,
To smooth the ice, or add another hue
Unto the rainbow, or with taper light
To seek the beauteous eye of heaven to garnish,
Is wasteful and ridiculous excess.

from *As You Like It*

All the world's a stage,
And all the men and women merely players:
They have their exits and their entrances;
And one man in his time plays many parts,
His acts being seven ages. At first the infant,
Mewling and puking in the nurse's arms.
And then the whining schoolboy, with his satchel,
And shining morning face, creeping like snail
Unwillingly to school. And then the lover,
Sighing like a furnace, with a woeful ballad
Made to his mistress' eyebrow. Then a soldier,
Full of strange oaths, and bearded like the pard,
Jealous in honour, sudden and quick in quarrel,
Seeking the bubble reputation
Even in the cannon's mouth. And then the justice,
In fair round belly with good capon lin'd,
With eyes severe, and beard of formal cut,
Full of wise saws and modern instances;
And so he plays his part. The sixth age shifts
Into the lean and slipper'd pantaloon,
With spectacles on nose and pouch on side,
His youthful hose well sav'd a world too wide
For his shrunk shank; and his big manly voice,
Turning again towards childish treble, pipes
And whistles in his sound. Last scene of all,
That ends this strange eventful history,
Is second childishness, and mere oblivion,
Sans teeth, sans eyes, sans taste, sans everything.

Index of First Lines

Index of Authors and Titles

Thomas Gray (1716-1835)
Elegy Written in a Country Churchyard

Felicia Hemans (1793-1835)
Casabianca
Ivan the Czar
The Child's First Grief

James Hogg (1770-1845)
A Boy's Song

Thomas Hood (1799-1845)
Bed-Time
I Remember, I Remember
The Death Bed

Lord Houghton (1809-1885)
Good Night and Good Morning

Leigh Hunt (1784-1859)
Abou Ben Adhem

Dr Edward Jenner (1749-1823)
Signs of Rain

John Keats (1795-1821)
Ode to Autumn

Charles Kingsley (1819-1875)
The Sands of Dee
Young and Old

Rudyard Kipling (1865-1936)
If
Land of our Birth

Henry Wadsworth Longfellow (1807-1882)
A Psalm of Life
Hiawatha's Childhood

Julius Caesar
King Henry VIII
Othello
Measure for Measure
King John

Frank Dempster Sherman (1860-1916)
Daisies

James Shirley (1596-1666)
Death, the Leveller

Robert Southey (1774-1843)
After Blenheim
The Scholar and his Books

Robert Louis Stevenson (1850-1894)
Escape at Bed-Time
Farewell to the Farm
From a Railway Carriage
My Shadow
Over the Sea to Skye
Requiem
The Moon
The Swing

Alfred Lord Tennyson (1809-1892)
Break, Break, Break
I Envy not in any Moods
Ring Out, Wild bells
The Brook
The Lady of Shalott
The May Queen
Crossing the Bar

William Makepeace Thackeray (1811-1863)
A Tragic Story

Francis Thompson (1859-1907)
Little Jesus

Henry Vaughan (1622-1695)
The Retreat

John Greenleaf Whittier (1807-1892)
Barbara Freitchie
Night in Winter

William Wordsworth (1770-1850)
Lucy Gray
She Dwelt Among the Untrodden Ways
The Daffodils
To the Cuckoo